D1703927

Meet Cree

Meet
A guide to the
Cree
language

H. Christoph Wolfart
Janet F. Carroll

New and completely revised edition

University of Nebraska Press
Lincoln and London

First published in Canada in 1973 by
The University of Alberta Press
Edmonton, Alberta, Canada

Second Edition, 1981

Published simultaneously in the U.S.A. by
University of Nebraska Press
901 North 17th Street
Lincoln, Nebraska 68588

copyright © The University of Alberta Press 1981

Library of Congress Cataloging in Publication Data
Wolfart, H.   Christoph.
        Meet Cree.
        Bibliography: p.
    1. Cree language-Grammar. I. Carroll, Janet F.,
joint author.   II. Title.
PM987.W58 1981   497'.3   80-54330
ISBN 0-8032-4716-8

Typesetting by
The Typeworks
Mayne Island, British Columbia

Printed by
John Deyell Company
Willowdale, Ontario

Contents

Preface   vii

Introduction   ix
   Language   x
   Linguistic Patterns   xiii
   Cree Dialects   xv

1   The Sounds of Cree   1
   Distinctive Sounds   1
   Writing Cree   2
   Vowels   5
   Consonants   7
   Semivowels   10
   Surface Variations   12

2   A Personal Indexing System: Grammatical Categories   14
   Number   15
   Gender   17
   Person   22
   Third Persons (Proximate and Obviative)   25
   Direction   27
   Summary and Abbreviations   32

3 The Shape of Words: Noun Inflection   33
　　The Outer Layer: Number and Obviation   35
　　　　Stem Types   38
　　　　Place-forms   40
　　　　Address-forms   41
　　The Inner Layer: Possession   42
　　　　Dependent Stems   45
　　Combining Both Layers: Third Person Possessors   47
　　Pronoun Inflection   52
　　Summary of Vowel Adjustment Rules   52

4 The Shape of Words: Verb Inflection   53
　　Agreement   55
　　Transitive and Intransitive Stems   58
　　The Four Major Verb Types   60
　　The Inflection of Intransitive Verbs   63
　　The Inflection of Transitive Verbs   67
　　The Major Modes   73

5 Words and Sentences   80
　　Word Shape versus Word Order   82
　　Verb and Noun Expressions   84
　　Words as Sentences   85

6 Literature   89
　　Literature without Writing   90
　　Cree Literature   91
　　Literary Form   92
　　The Texts   93

Conclusion   106

Appendix: Supplementary Readings   107
　　Practical Works   107
　　Linguistics and Language Learning   110
　　More Technical Works on Cree   112
　　Difficulties with Books on Cree   114

Preface

Cree is the most widely spoken indigenous language of Canada.

As an introduction to the major features of the Cree language, this book responds first of all to a practical need: to explore the structure of Cree, to compare it with that of English, and to identify some of the difficulties that speakers of either language experience in learning to speak the other.

An encounter with another language is an aesthetic experience which often goes unrecognized. Like art, language is a prominent medium of cultural expression—as seen in the rich traditional literature of the Cree. But the beauty which lies in the complex structure of language itself is easily overshadowed by practical difficulties. This sketch, in spite of its extremely limited scope, is intended to offer a first glance at the intricacies of the Cree language.

The first edition of this book, published in 1973, was addressed mainly to teachers, nurses, and other Euro-Canadians who live and work in Cree-speaking communities; it was also widely used, we were gratified to discover, in courses on the structure of Cree and as background reading in spoken language programs. While the needs of these two audiences have remained our primary concern in this revised and expanded edition, we have also kept in mind a third: the general reader who may turn to a brief book on the Cree language simply from curiosity.

We are grateful to our friends and colleagues, speakers of both Cree and English, who have in various ways contributed to this book.

Winnipeg, Manitoba
December 1978

Introduction

This is a book *about* Cree; it will not teach you to speak Cree. No book alone can do that, for language learning requires practice in several skills: listening to Cree sounds and producing those which have no counterpart in English, forming Cree words and putting them together into sentences, and, finally, using the sentences in new kinds of social situations. Such skills are best taught in the classroom or by a tutor.

To recognize the differences which exist between Cree and English is not only useful in learning to speak Cree. Some of the misunderstandings which arise in cross-cultural situations might well be avoided if there were a greater awareness of language differences.

Knowing something about how a language works is not the same as the ability to speak and understand it. But without some knowledge of the structural plan of Cree, the practical task of language learning would be much more difficult.

Before we can look at Cree, however, we need to take note of some features that all languages share on the following pages.

Language

Speech is a distinctly human ability. Even though certain animals, dolphins for example, are able to communicate with one another to some degree, only human beings can go beyond set messages and the here and now.

We can describe situations which have not been experienced by those who listen. We can create completely new sentences to frame our story. We can talk about events that did not take place (such as *My car didn't start, The bus was late,* or similar lies of convenience), and we even have words for things that do not exist (such as *unicorn* or *Martian*). And we can create words for novel things: both Cree and German, as it happens, came up with words meaning 'flying-thing' when they first needed a term for an artificial bird: Cree *pimibākan,* German *Flugzeug.*

When we get tired of our immediate situation, we can talk about things that happened long ago and send verbal signals to one another about events that are yet to take place. Man alone in the animal world can communicate about things and events outside his immediate environment.

Sharing this uniquely human ability, every society in the world has a language, and some are lucky enough to have more than one. We work, play, raise children, share happiness and troubles – all with language. Language not only is the means by which we carry on the daily activities of our society in a particular slice of time; it also ties together succeeding generations. Children everywhere learn the language of their parents, and they learn it in an incredibly short time. Every five-year-old has mastered most of the language structures he or she will need for a lifetime of talking.

Of course, the thousands of languages around the world differ, sometimes drastically, in their sounds (and in many other ways as well). Hearing a foreign language spoken is a baffling experience since its sounds appear to be no more than a jumble of noises. The speaker of the other language, however, has no difficulty in keeping them apart, while your language, in turn, sounds equally unintelligible to him.

Differences between languages rarely "make sense"; it is not a matter of reason or logic that English speakers put their adjectives before nouns, as in *Red River,* and speakers of French put them after nouns, as in *Rivière Rouge,* but of linguistic habit. Languages simply are different.

Languages also tend to reflect the preoccupations of a particular culture.

In Arabic, for example, there are many words referring to camels — consider their crucial rôle in traditional desert life — and their parts, whereas the one word, *camel*, suffices for the needs of most English speakers. A highly mechanized society, on the other hand, demands dozens of words for *their* favourite mode of transportation and its parts: *piston, spark-plug, tie-rod, distributor*, etc. Even within one society, not everyone uses the same level of detail in his or her vocabulary; those who make do without a car or know a reliable mechanic may never have to learn the specialized meaning of *valve-job*. Ordinary city-dwellers will not recognize terms such as *heifer*, which are common enough in the barnyard, and even in Canada a zoo-keeper may have a fancy camel-vocabulary.

Important matters, it seems, deserve words of their own. But there are other, less obvious indications that our native tongue is not entirely independent of the way we look at the world. Our sense of time, for example, is usually expressed through language. In English verb forms such as *he was/is/will be walking*, the most prominent feature is a division of time into three discrete parts: past, present, and future. The basic distinction among Russian verb forms, on the other hand, depends on whether the action is complete or incomplete.

Even such seemingly "real" and unalterable things as colours are classified differently in different languages: the Welsh word *glas*, for instance, covers English *blue* and part of the ranges of *green* and *grey* as well:

English	*green*	*blue*	*grey*
Welsh		*glas*	

Kin relationships present another case. The English word *uncle* applies to the brother of either parent. In Cree or in Latin, on the other hand, the two types of uncles are not lumped together:

	'father's brother'	'mother's brother'
English	*uncle*	
Cree	*nōhcāwīs* or *nōhkomis*	*nisis*
Latin	*patruus*	*avunculus*

This does not mean that speakers of Welsh are colour-blind or that English speakers cannot tell the difference between "Uncle Jim, you know, the one on my mother's side" and "Uncle Joe who was my dad's brother." These examples merely show that there is a great deal of diversity among the languages of mankind.

Despite very real differences, however, all languages are much the same in complexity and effectiveness. In any language man can make generalizations (*trees*) or discriminations (*white spruce* or *tamarack*); we can refer by means of word-symbols to physical things like dogs or less tangible ideas such as beauty or democracy. In all languages, people can say whatever needs to be expressed in that society. What is more, languages can adjust to new requirements. When the need arose in the Arab-speaking world to have more names for the parts of automobiles and oil-pumps, the new terms were created easily enough.

Societies obviously differ in the extent of their technological development, but that does *not* mean that their respective languages vary accordingly in complexity or capability. The language of people who find skyscrapers important enough to agree on a special word-label for them is not one bit more sophisticated than the language of people who build grass huts or igloos instead. Members of a so-called "primitive" society do not speak a "primitive" language—far from it.

In discussing language we emphasize speech rather than writing because it is the more fundamental of the two: writing is secondary, a mere reflection of speech. Even students and teachers usually spend far more time each day talking than writing, and as children we all were able to speak long before we learned to make recognizable marks on paper. Looking around us, we find that every group of people uses a spoken form of language, but many societies—in fact the majority—manage quite well with no system of written signs at all. Historically, men (and women too, of course) began to talk to one another centuries before they carved symbolic squiggles onto stones.

Linguistic Patterns

Perhaps the most important trait of language to be examined here is the fact that it is a **system**.

In all languages words are made up of consonants and vowels. Just how many consonants can be clustered together without a vowel in between varies from language to language, but it is always a definite pattern. In English, for example, we can have *rsts* at the end of a word (as in *bursts*) but certainly not at the beginning. Similarly, there are words like *sue* and *zoo* and *shoe*—but no English word begins with *zh* (as in *confusion*). Even simple clusters are not free to occur just anywhere. We use *ts* in *hats* or *cats* but never at the beginning of a word: most people pronounce **ts***etse-fly* as if it were written "*tetse-fly.*"

The forms of words fall into patterns which are much easier to recognize than those of sounds. All English verbs, for example, share at least these three forms:

they	*sing,*	*laugh,*	*dance*
they are	*sing-ing,*	*laugh-ing,*	*danc-ing*
he/she	*sing-s,*	*laugh-s,*	*dance-s*

These forms have technical names, to be sure, but it is sufficient to note that the verb which follows *he/she* always has an *s*-like sound added to it, that no such sound ever occurs when the verb follows *they*, and that all verbs add *-ing* when they are used with *is/are*.

We can observe the common structure of English verbs even in those cases where the individual forms differ. In the past tenses, for example, most verbs add *-ed* but some do not; instead, they use a different vowel, as in *sang* or *swam:*

> *they sang, laugh-ed, dance-d*

In spite of the differing forms, however, we can see the same relation between

> *sing* and *sang,*
> *laugh* and *laughed,*
> *dance* and *danced,*

etc.

When words are put together to form sentences, they are again combined systematically. Starting from the examples below, any speaker of English could add new sentences of the same structure without ever stopping:

John	*likes*		*apples.*
The bearded old carpenter	*ate*	*an entire three-course*	*dinner.*
A bald soprano	*swallowed*	*rotten*	*eggs.*
Two gnomes	*were trying to console*	*the crying*	*child.*

The columns correspond to word classes such as noun, verb, and adjective, and their rôles in the sentence are traditionally known by such terms as subject, object, predicate. But as our example shows, we can recognize the pattern and form new sentences from it without looking at the technical terms.

The emphasis on *system* in language will be our guiding theme throughout this book. We cannot always manage without technical terms, and in many situations they are useful (sometimes indispensable) as labels for a specific set of examples. But the pattern of actual forms is always more important than the label, and we have tried to give enough examples for the pattern to be recognized.

Sounds are the building blocks from which all utterances are constructed, so we begin our survey of Cree with the sound system. Before we can explore the systematic nature of Cree sounds, however, we need to discuss the issue of Cree dialects; for the local flavour of a language is largely carried by its sounds—in Montréal or Marseille French as in the English of

London or New Orleans.

Once we have presented the sound system and discussed the orthography used in this book, we can go on to the very general features which are found in both nouns and verbs; for example, the grammatical category of number which appears in such singular and plural forms as *cat : cats* or *he sings : they sing*. Chapters three and four are concerned with the make-up of words while chapter five explores the relationship between words and sentences. Further works about Cree are reviewed in the Appendix.

People do not always speak in sentences. On some occasions we use broken-off pieces of sentences, on others we try to tie a number of sentences together into a paragraph-like structure. The texts of chapter six are examples of connected speech — and of traditional Cree literature.

Cree Dialects

What is "the Cree language"? First of all, even though people often refer to their own language as "the Indian language" this expression must not be taken too literally. There is no one "Indian" language which would be common to all Indians, just as there is no one "White Man's language." Terms of this kind make sense only within a particular region.

In fact, in spite of considerable language loss in North America, well over a hundred indigenous languages are still spoken today, and they may be as different from one another as English is from, say, Japanese.

There are four major dialects of modern Cree: **Plains Cree, Swampy Cree, Woods Cree,** and **Moose Cree.** The map shows the various regions in which these dialects are spoken today; in reality, however, the boundaries are much fuzzier than the clear lines on the map suggest on the following page.

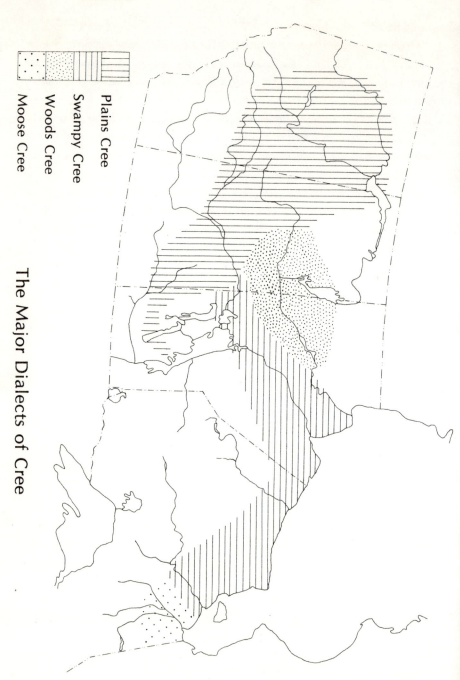

Plains Cree
Swampy Cree
Woods Cree
Moose Cree

The Major Dialects of Cree

The dialects of the Cree language differ in a few sounds and in occasional words, but the differences are relatively minor. Let us look at one word as it appears in the several dialects:

> 'I'
>
> *nīya*   Plains Cree
> *nīna*   Swampy Cree
> *nīθa*   Woods Cree
> *nīla*   Moose Cree

The only difference between these words is a single sound: a *y* in Plains Cree corresponds to an *n* in Swampy Cree, a *θ* in Woods Cree,* and an *l* in Moose Cree. It is this systematic correspondence of *y-n-θ-l* which sets apart the four major dialects of Cree. To take another example:

> 'I like him/her'
> *nimiywēyimāw*   Plains Cree
> *niminwēnimāw*   Swampy Cree
> *nimiθwēθimāw*   Woods Cree
> *nimilwēlimāw*   Moose Cree

Aside from this variation of *y-n-θ-l*, the dialects of Cree share many common features and a Cree speaker from one dialect community can generally understand a speaker from a neighbouring region, just as an English speaker from Winnipeg can communicate quite easily with a native of Chicago.

In English, French, and other European languages there is usually one dialect which has more prestige than the others. In formal situations, for example, the BBC type of English is regarded as more elegant or more educated than regional dialect, and even in Canada some people try to say *new* to rhyme with *cue* rather than with *too* (an effort which often will merely make them sound silly). In a similar fashion, schoolteachers tend to

---

*θ (called *theta*) is pronounced much like the *th* in the English *the* or *although*; in other books it is occasionally spelled *th*, *dh*, or *ð*.

regard Parisian French as their model and to look down upon normal Canadian French; there are many French speakers, on the other hand, who make a point of *not* sounding like a Parisian.

Cree speakers do not have the problem of choosing "the correct way to speak." Unlike those languages where one dialect is preferred over the others and recognized as "standard," Cree is equally "proper" when spoken in each and every one of its regional variants.

Plains Cree and Swampy Cree are the most widely spoken dialects: together they account for at least three-quarters of the total number of about sixty-thousand Cree speakers. Most of the examples in this book will fit Plains Cree and Swampy Cree equally well.

The major exception is the use of *y* in Plains Cree and of *n* in Swampy Cree in the type of words we have illustrated above. To indicate this sound we use a special symbol, *ý*. The letter *y* with an acute accent mark, *'*, thus indicates the Plains Cree *y* which corresponds to Swampy Cree *n*, Woods Cree *θ*, and Moose Cree *l*.

From this point on, therefore, the Plains Cree words for 'I' and 'I like him/her' will be written *nīýa* and *nimiýwēýimāw*. With this special symbol, if we come across a Plains Cree form such as

> *ka-mīýitin* 'I will give it to you,'

we can predict that in the Swampy Cree region the same form will be

> *ka-mīnitin.*

Similarly,

	'it goes well'	
	miýopaýiw	Plains Cree
	minopaniw	Swampy Cree
	miθopaθiw	Woods Cree
	milopaliw	Moose Cree
or		
	'it is windy'	
	ýōtin	Plains Cree
	nōtin	Swampy Cree
	θōtin	Woods Cree
	lōtin	Moose Cree

This special *ý* of Plains Cree can be recognized only when looked at from the point of view of another dialect. Within Plains Cree, it sounds exactly like the ordinary *y* which is matched by *y* in Swampy Cree and the other two dialects:

'one'
pēyak	Plains Cree
pēyak	Swampy Cree
pēyak	Woods Cree
pēyak	Moose Cree

Contrast two words with the two *y*-symbols of Plains Cree:

'it is difficult'	'properly, straight'	
āýiman	*kwayask*	Plains Cree
āniman	*kwayask*	Swampy Cree
āθiman	*kwayask*	Woods Cree
āliman	*kwayask*	Moose Cree

The use of *ý*, *n*, *θ*, and *l* in certain words is the simplest way of telling Cree dialects apart. It is not the only feature, however, which varies from region to region and distinguishes the dialects. In northern Alberta and Saskatchewan, for example, the first vowel of *pēyak* will sound like that of *niýa;* in many areas of Manitoba, Swampy Cree has *miscēt* 'many' instead of the more common *mihcēt*. Where a Cree speaker from central Alberta says *ē-apicik* 'as they sit,' someone from northern Alberta would say *ē-apitwāw*. And, of course, the dialects sometimes use different words; while central Alberta Cree, for example, has *ōsi* for 'canoe,' most of the other dialects use *cīmān*. These more localized dialect variations which are found in many communities are confusing when you read about them in a book — and they would take a fairly massive book to describe them all. Fortunately, they are quite easy to learn on the spot.

Finally, there are several other languages (for instance Ojibwa or Saulteau) which are closely related to Cree. Just as German *hundert* is similar in sound to English *hundred* (and identical in meaning), so Cree *pōsiw* 'he embarks, gets aboard' is similar to Ojibwa *pōsi* and so Cree *nipāw* 'he sleeps' matches Ojibwa *nipā*. Similarities like these give an impression of familiarity which is quite deceptive; they are the exception rather than the rule. Cree and Ojibwa are distinct, separate languages whose speakers cannot understand one another any more than the speakers of English can understand German. Yet Cree is more similar to Ojibwa than either is to English. From a wider perspective, the basic structural plans of closely related languages are remarkably similar.

1   The Sounds of Cree

In speaking about **sounds** we mean the real, audible sounds of a language; that is, we mean neither the *letters* used to represent these sounds in writing (*a*, *b*, *c*, and so on) nor the *names* of these letters (for instance, the name "bee" for *b* or the name "eye" for *i*). Only some languages have been written down with letters, but all languages have sounds.

The sounds of a language can be approached from two perspectives. The first is to take note of all the minute sound variations which occur in normal speech; their number is extremely large. The second is to describe only those sounds that are *distinctive* — in other words, only the sounds which are sufficiently different from other sounds to signal a difference in meaning. The second is a less ambitious task perhaps, yet more useful, and our study of Cree will chiefly take this second approach. However, an English example of the first kind of description may help us to understand both more clearly.

Distinctive Sounds

Try saying these two words aloud:
> *pin : spin*

You will notice that there is a slight difference between the *p*-sound in *pin*, which is immediately followed by a small puff of air, and the *p*-sound in *spin*, which is not. (To **see** the difference between these two sounds, say *spin* and *pin* while holding a lighted match in front of your lips. The extra explosion of breath in *pin* should put out the match.) Yet these two variants of the *p*-sound could be interchanged without the meaning of either word being affected: if you said *spin* with the breathy *p* of *pin*, you would still be understood.

On the other hand, if you said *bin* instead of *pin*, obviously you would be talking about something quite different. Contrast in sound indicates a difference of meaning here, so we say that the sounds *p* and *b* are **distinctive** in English.

In studying Cree we must recognize that the patterns of English, these familiar ways of telling bits of speech apart, are not always the same ones used to differentiate sounds in another language. It is as though we had to "shift gears" mentally as we listen to Cree in order to become attuned to its particular patterns. This is not to say that English and Cree have totally dissimilar sound systems, for the two languages do share a number of individual sounds and distinctions. Nevertheless, English speakers must lay aside some familiar distinctions and learn a few new ones.

Writing Cree

Before we go on we should return once more to the problem of sounds and letters and the names we use for them.

We all know the discrepancies which exist between the spoken word and its written forms. English offers a wealth of examples since the traditional English orthography is far removed from the actual sound system of English.

One sound may be represented by different symbols, as in
>*wi**n**dow*
>*w**o**men;*

or
>*nati**o**nal,*
>*fashi**o**nable,*
>*fi**sh**;*

or

    the book you sent me,

    not another cent,

    the scent of wild flowers.

Conversely, the same letter or sequence of letters may stand for several different sounds:

    a northerly wind   (same sound as in *window*)

    these roads wind a lot   (same sound as in *wine*)

or

    he likes to read   (same sound as in *reed*)

    he read the book   (same sound as in *red*)

    his heart   (same sound as in *hard*)

In

    *enou*gh

and

    *throu*gh,

the same letter-sequence *gh* is written for the sound *f* and for nothing at all. Since sounds and letters do not match, the writing system of English is extremely difficult to learn and use—even for children (and adults!) who speak English natively.

Obviously, this kind of inconsistency is best avoided. Cree as written in this book uses *the same symbol for each distinctive sound* each time that sound is put into writing. This method, which has enormous practical advantages, is also known as the principle of **one sound, one letter.**

Instead of looking back at the all-too-familiar complications of English spelling, we should treat Cree writing on its own terms. In some contexts, this may mean the use of **syllabic** characters such as

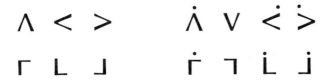

But there are others where the characters of the **Roman alphabet** offer a practical alternative. These letters are not, after all, wedded to English; they are used for a host of diverse languages. So long as they are used in a way

which fits the Cree language, they readily serve as **Cree letters for Cree sounds**.

Once Roman letters have been turned into Cree letters, confusion may still be caused by the names which are often given to English letters. If someone speaks, for example, about

"the sound 'i',"

what is meant? The sound of

eye

or that of

window?

In terms of Cree, would he/she mean the first sound of

ay-api 'sit down!'

or that of

iskotēw 'fire'?

This confusion is easily avoided if we stay away from the English labels for sounds and letters. Instead, we can simply use a special *keyword* for each Cree letter—and, of course, also for the one and only sound this letter represents. We can then refer to *a* as the **a***stotin*-vowel or to *n* as the **n***iska*-sound, and so on:

i*skwēsis*
a*stotin*
o*spwākan*

s*īsīp*
m*ēskanaw*
n*āpēw*
m*ōswa*

p*akān*
t*ēpakohp*
c*īkahikan*
k*inēpik*
s*ikāk*
a*hāsiw*
m*ōhkomān*
n*iska*

wāpos
pēyak

If these new terms seem awkward at first, remember that we can avoid a great deal of confusion by using **Cree names for Cree sounds**.

Vowels

Cree has seven vowel sounds, three short and four long:*

short	long
i	*ī*
	ē
a	*ā*
o	*ō*

In this book, long vowels are written with a horizontal bar** placed above the letter.

The length of vowels is primarily a matter of *time:* a **long** vowel lasts longer than a **short** vowel. Whatever other differences exist are of the non-distinctive kind.

The distinction of vowel length in Cree serves to keep words apart:

sakahikan

and

sākahikan

---

*With respect to vowels, the terms *short* and *long* have a technical meaning which is defined below. It is unfortunate that English dictionaries sometimes use the expression "long vowel" in another sense which is not the same at all. The vowel of *made*, for example, is no *longer* than that of *mad*; it is simply **different**.

** This bar is also known as a **macron**. For typing simplicity, other symbols have also been used in writing Cree: a vowel letter followed by a raised dot (*o·*) or by a colon (*o:*), double vowel symbols (*oo*), or an acute accent (*ó*).

These words differ only in the length of the first vowel, but they are distinct and mean completely different things:

> *sakahikan*   'nail'
> *sākahikan*   'lake'

Other examples:

> *asam*   'feed him!'
> *asām*   'snowshoe'
>
> *nipiy*   'water'
> *nīpiy*   'leaf'
>
> *askihk*   'kettle, pail'
> *askīhk*   'on the earth'

The three short vowels of Cree are reasonably similar to the vowels of English *bin*, *but*, and *foot*. For the long vowels, on the other hand, the English illustrations are, at best, rough approximations:

Cree vowels	as in	*roughly* as in English
short:		
i	*iskwēsis* 'girl'	*bin*
a	*astotin* 'cap'	*but*
o	*ospwākan* 'pipe'	*foot*
long:		
ī	*sīsīp* 'duck'	*bean*
ē	*mēskanaw* 'road'	*pain*
ā	*nāpēw* 'man, adult'	*barn*
ō	*mōswa* 'moose'	*bone*

These vowels do not, of course, always sound exactly the same; the quality of the short vowels, for instance, is most easily distinguished when they are stressed. The vowels also vary somewhat depending on the dialect, with *ē* the most extreme example: in some dialect areas (notably in northern Saskatchewan), the *ē* of *mēskanaw* sounds exactly like the *ī* of *sīsīp*.

The standard illustrations of the short and long vowels of Cree—and the best ones to remember—are their own Cree names. Note that those for *short* vowels have the vowel at the beginning of the word, for instance *iskwēsis*; the names for *long* vowels purposely have the vowel preceded by a consonant, as in *sīsīp*.

Further examples of the vowels follow:

i *iskotēw* 'fire'	*atim* 'dog'	*api* 'sit down!'
a *asām* 'snowshoe'	*masinahikan* 'paper, book'	*maskwa* 'bear'
o *okimāw* 'boss, chief'	*sihkos* 'weasel'	*nikamo* 'sing!'

ī *ītawiyaw* 'at both sides'	*nisīm* 'my younger brother'	*kocī* 'try!'
ē *ēskan* 'horn'	*mihcēt* 'many'	*mētawē* 'play!'
ā *āpihtaw* 'half'	*mōhkomān* 'knife'	*nipā* 'sleep!'
ō *ōhōw* 'owl'	*nimosōm* 'my grandfather'	*pasikō* 'get up!'

Consonants

All dialects* of Cree have the following consonants:

*Some of the eastern dialects have *s* and *š*, which is like the first sound of the English sh*oe*, instead of the one sound *s* which occurs in the western dialects; for example, they have *sākahikan* 'lake' but *šīšīp* 'duck.' Moose Cree also has *l*, as in *lōtin* 'it is windy,' and Woods Cree has θ as in *θōtin* 'it is windy.'

Cree
consonant   as in

p	p*akān* 'nut'
t	t*ēpakohp* 'seven'
c	c*īkahikan* 'axe'
k	k*inēpik* 'snake'
s	s*ikāk* 'skunk'
h	ah*āsiw* 'crow'
m	m*ōhkomān* 'knife'
n	n*iska* 'goose'

If we compare the first four consonants, *p*, *t*, *c*, and *k*, with their English counterparts, we find that the distinction of **voicing**, which is very important for English consonants, is not made at all in Cree. In English, voicing* marks the only difference between pairs of words that otherwise sound identical, as in these examples:

p*in* : b*in*   t*in* : d*in*   k*ill* : g*ill*

c*a*p : c*a*b   p*a*t : p*a*d   p*ick* : p*ig*

Since this distinction does not exist in Cree, an English speaker must not be alarmed if he or she hears variants of *t* in Cree that seem more like *d*—or even like a sound half-way between the two; these variations do not signal a difference in meaning. (Such variations sometimes occur in English, too, where meaning *is* affected: if you hear someone say the word *bitter* without a full sentence accompanying it, you may not be sure whether they said *bitter* or *bidder*.)

*To get a clearer understanding of what *voicing* (vibration of the vocal chords) means, try holding your "Adam's apple" and saying the first sound in the word *pack*: *p-p-p-p*. Now, keep your hand in the same position and say *b-b-b-b* as in *bag*, and you will feel a buzzing movement in your throat.

When *p, t,* and *k* appear at the beginning or end of a Cree word, they sound much like their counterparts (that is, the voiceless *p, t,* and *k*) in English. In the middle of a word, however, when they are surrounded by vowels, the impression given by Cree *p, t,* and *k* often is more like that of the voiced *b, d,* and *g* of English.

As the first or last sound of a word, the Cree sound represented by the letter *c* (that is, the *cīkahikan*-sound) is similar to the *ts* at the end of English *pats,* for instance *mēkwāc* 'in the meantime.' In the middle of a word, as in *mīciwin* 'food,' it resembles the final sound of English *pads.* The *cīkahikan*-sound is not, however, always the same as these English sounds: its pronunciation may range from the last sounds of *pats* and *pads* all the way to those of *rich* and *ridge.* Now, a look at the sound system of English tells us that the sounds at the end of *rich* and *ridge* are also heard at the beginning of *chill* and *Jill.* But the same is not true for the sounds at the end of *pats* and *pads,* which in English never occur at the beginning of a word! English speakers may find it difficult, therefore, to produce the familiar sound of *pats* in unfamiliar surroundings (unless, of course, they happen to talk about *tsetse-flies* a lot). Clearly, we need to pay attention not only to the individual sounds but also to their position within the word.

The Cree consonants *p, t, c,* and *k* also offer a good example of distinctions which are made in Cree but not in English. In this case, again, the two languages differ not so much in the sounds themselves as in the way the sounds are arranged. For although neither language recognizes a distinctive difference between *p*-sounds that are followed by a small explosion of air, and those that are not, Cree *does* distinguish between *p*-sounds that are *preceded* by a little puff of air and those that are not. This also applies for the sounds of *t, c,* and *k,* where this breathiness before the consonant signals a difference in meaning. For example, notice the distinction between the *t* and the *ht* in these words:

> *ē-wāpamit* 'when he sees me'
> *ē-wāpamiht* 'when he is seen'

or in

> *wīcihik* 'help me!'
> *wīcihihk* 'help him!'

As is suggested by the spelling here, we can think of the **pre-aspirated** forms of these consonants as being sounds with an *h* in front of them. Making this distinction will seem unusual to English speakers, just as some sound combinations in English strike a Cree speaker as strange. Neither language is better or "easier" than the other; they are simply *different*.

In short, students of another language will have to *learn* some new distinctions which are not made in their own and *unlearn* other, familiar ones which are not found in their new language. Just as Cree speakers learning to speak English should concentrate on the distinction between, for example, *pat* and *pad* or between *my kit* and *my kid*, so English speakers need practice in recognizing the pre-aspirated and simple forms of *p, t, c,* and *k*.

The remaining consonants of Cree are pronounced much like their English counterparts, no matter where in the word they come. The *abāsiw*-sound (that is, *h*) is distinctive only when it occurs within a word; the *h*-like noise often heard at the beginning or end of words (see page 13) is a sign of the word boundary.

Examples of each Cree consonant in the various positions in which it may occur are given throughout this chapter. There are also illustrations of some consonant clusters, such as

> *hp, ht, hc,* and *hk,*

or

> *sk,*
> *skw,*

and so forth. Further examples may be found in later chapters and especially in the texts of chapter six. As you look at these examples, you should always remember that the comparisons with English sounds are crude approximations **at best**. No book can replace a tutor who actually speaks the language.

Semivowels

In Cree as in English, semivowels differ from both vowels and consonants. They usually appear as glides, that is, always together with a vowel; note the sound (not merely the letter) *y* in the English words *you* and *music* and in *joy, join, joyous.*

The two semivowels of Cree are pronounced much like their English counterparts:

Cree
semivowel   as in

   w   *wāpos* 'rabbit'
   y   *pēyak* 'one'

In pronouncing *w*, Cree speakers round their lips less than English speakers do for their *w*. The lip-rounding is still enough, however, to affect neighbouring vowels which become more *o*-like when preceded or followed by *w*.

Cree semivowels typically occur directly after a consonant, as the last member of a consonant cluster:

   kw*ayask*   'properly, straight'
   kīkway   'what'

   pahkwēsikan   'bannock'
   iskwēw   'woman'

But they may also stand by themselves:

   ýēkaw   'sand'
   kisēýiniw   'old man'
   watay   'his belly'

When appearing at the beginning or end of a word or between vowels, semivowels occupy the same position as consonants.

Surface Variations

In discussing individual sounds, in Cree as in any other language, we tend to treat them as perfectly stable units which sound exactly the same whenever they are used. In fact, however, they vary not only from speaker to speaker but also from one neighbouring sound to another. In any language, there are **surface variations** scattered around the ideal sound targets.

Their effect is easily seen if we compare the careful mouthing of individual words or the enunciation style of the stage with speech produced at its natural pace. In normal, everyday English it is quite common to hear a later sound anticipated in an earlier one. In *this year*, for instance, many English speakers get ready for the *y* just a split-second too soon and end up saying *thish year* instead. The influence that the Cree *w* has on neighbouring vowels is quite similar: in *apiw* 'he sits,' for instance, the *i* often sounds more like an *o* because the lips get ready for the *w* immediately after the *p*.

As we speak more quickly, perhaps excitedly, some sounds may be lost entirely; many English speakers make *government*, for example, a two-syllable word, "gubment." Whole words may be run together, as in this meal-time conversation:

A. "Djeet?"   (with "dj" almost as in *Jim*)

B. "Djoo?"

In the standard orthography of English,

A. *Did you eat?*

B. *Did you?*

seem familiar enough.

In normal speech, the final vowels of Cree words may merge with the initial vowel of the next word:

nāpēw mīna atim   'a man and a dog'

can be reduced to

nāpēw mīn ātim.

The result of this contraction is that the *a* becomes long, *ā*; it is as though two short *a*'s equalled one long one. If different vowels follow each other, the first is dropped and the second is lengthened:

nāpēw mīna iskwēw 'a man and a woman'

nāpēw mīn iskwēw

The contraction need not take place: vowels may simply follow each other, as in
mīna iskwēw,
or they may be separated by an *h*-like sound (see page 10) whose only function is to indicate the word boundary:
mīna(h) *iskwēw*
In this area, there is a variety of options which can be sorted out only after a good deal of listening practice.

Even within a word, short vowels may disappear if they are unstressed; this is particularly common between *s* and *t* or between *n* and *s:*

*ki*nisit*ohtawin cī*   'do you understand me?'
*ki*nst*ohtawin cī*

The first is slow, deliberate speech, the second more rapid, normal speech. Similarly:

*tā*nis*i*   'how; how are you (as a greeting)'
*tā*ns*i*

Once a vowel has vanished, the sounds which have been thrown together may further influence one another. In
nikī-nipān 'I had slept,'
the loss of the two short *i*'s leaves the two *n*'s standing directly in front of a *k* and a *p:*
n*kī*-n*pān*
As a result, we may hear them as *ng* (the sound of English *si*ng) and *m:*
n*gkī*-m*pān*
Anyone listening to Cree or English spoken at a natural speed will encounter surface variations, and some of them may make a word or a phrase difficult to understand. But they are only a surface problem — like the tip of an iceberg. While they must be recognized, they should not distract our attention from the basic structures which lie beneath the surface.

2 A Personal Indexing System: Grammatical Categories

Sound distinctions keep words apart. If someone utters either of these questions,

>   *Where is my ca*p*?*

or

>   *Where is my ca*b*?*

we need to know nothing about the speaker's circumstances: the voicing contrast between English *p* and *b* alone will be enough to tell us whether he is looking for his hat or waiting for a taxi.

In longer stretches of speech, which reflect more complicated situations, grammatical distinctions help us keep track of who or what is being discussed. In the following report, the distinction of *he* and *she* picks up the earlier distinction of *a man* and *a woman*:

>   *As I came closer, I saw a man and a woman;*
>   *he was chopping wood and she was carrying water.*

As speakers and listeners alike, we rely on grammatical categories, such as gender, number, person, tense, voice,etc. to tell or be told who does what to whom.

The system of **grammatical categories** might be viewed as the general framework of a language. The categories which the next few sections will introduce in some detail play an essential rôle in the make-up of nouns and verbs and in the way nouns and verbs are combined into sentences.

Everyone accepts the fact that languages do not all sound the same, yet we know that there are substantial similarities between sound systems in spite of the differences. The same is true of grammatical systems. Cree and English are similar, for example, in the category of number: they both distinguish singular, as in *he*, and plural, as in *they*. This simple distinction may seem obvious and natural to speakers of Cree or English but many languages (for example, Classical Greek) make special allowance for things that come in pairs such as eyes, ears, or the handles on a pot.

Although Cree and English both pay attention to gender as a grammatical category of nouns (such as *man* or *woman*), gender distinctions in Cree also extend to verbs. But the most striking difference in this area is that, as categories of *linguistic* structure, the gender distinctions of Cree and English are not based on the same *natural* feature.

Even the experience of familiar material being rearranged into new patterns is repeated among the grammatical categories. The persons which appear in a simple scene or conversation are the same in both languages—*I*, *you*, and a *third person* which is neither I nor you. But when they are put together into groups, Cree and English arrange them into different combinations.

Grammatical categories such as gender, number, or person are essential aspects of every sentence. When they are used normally, we hardly know they exist. But we are startled by the unexpected—by the telling cry of the suffragettes, for instance:

Pray to God, **She'll** *understand!*

Number

In English as in Cree, the grammatical category of **number** is found in nouns, pronouns, and verbs. The words *cat, dog,* and *child* normally refer to a single cat, a single dog, a single child; the words *cats, dogs,* and *children,* on the other hand, refer to any number of cats, dogs, and children so long as there are at least two of them. The word *cat* is **singular,** the word *cats* is **plural.**

Verbs, too, show contrasting forms for singular and plural, and these vary along with the singular and plural forms of nouns and pronouns:

>*this dog barks a lot* : *these dogs bark a lot*
>*he runs fast*   : *they run fast*
>*he is hungry*   : *they are hungry*

Most English verbs show the distinction of number only in the third person of the present tense (and there are some, like *can, must,* and so forth, which never show it):

>*the child sings* : *the children sing*

but

>*I dance*   : *we dance*

or

>*I laughed*   : *we laughed*

The distinction is still there, of course, in *I dance : we dance,* but it is expressed by the pronouns *I* and *we* rather than through the verb forms.

As we have already seen, Cree and English match in the number distinction itself: singular versus plural. But they are also similar in the way the number distinction is expressed in nouns. In both languages, the plural of a noun is formed by adding a special ending to the singular:

>*duck* : *duck*s
>*sīsīp* : *sīsīp*ak

There are, of course, always exceptions and complications. English has plurals like *man : men, foot : feet* and in some cases no special plural ending at all, as in *one sheep : two sheep*. In Cree it is also not enough to simply add *-ak* to any noun—just as no fluent speaker of English would claim *to stand on his own two foots*. In chapter three we will look at similar problems in Cree, such as nouns where a *w* appears between the form of the singular and the plural ending:

> *atim*   'dog'
> *atim*w*ak*   'dogs'

For the moment, however, we concentrate on number as a general category rather than discussing the various plural endings of nouns, pronouns, and verbs in detail.

The *use* of the number distinction shows a third parallel between Cree and English. The singular, for instance, may be used for general statements:

> *Man is a political animal.*

> *ohtitaw ta-pāhpit aýīsiýiniw.*
> 'People will always laugh.'

Both the noun *aýīsiýiniw* 'person' and the verb *ta-pāhpit* 'he will laugh' are singular.

In Cree and English alike, finally, singular nouns and pronouns **agree** with singular verbs, and plural nouns and pronouns **agree** with plural verbs:

> *this duck* **is** *sleeping*
> *these duck*s **arc** *sleeping*

> *awa sīsīp   nipāw*
> *ōki   sīsīp*ak *nipāw*ak

The agreement between the plural noun *sīsīp*ak 'ducks' and the plural verb form *nipāw*ak 'they sleep' is most obvious because of the shared ending -*ak*. The same agreement exists—less visible perhaps but no less real—between *awa/this* and *sīsīp/duck* as between *ōki/these* and *sīsīpak/ducks*.

Gender

Very few English nouns show the gender distinction by an overt ending such as the *-ess* of *steward*ess or *princ*ess. But we can easily enough tell the gender of nouns by substituting the personal pronoun *he, she,* or *it* for the noun itself.

In many cases, the **grammatical gender** of a noun corresponds directly to the biological sex of the person or animal to which the noun refers: the words *uncle* or *bull* are **masculine** and uncles or bulls are male, just as grandmothers or female horses are represented by the **feminine** words *grandmother* or *mare*. A similar correspondence is found with proper names like *John* or *Mary;* but some names are as ambiguous as many common nouns, and neither the name nor the descriptive phrase reveals that

> *the English novelist Evelyn Waugh*

is, in fact, a man. In North American usage, *Evelyn* is primarily a woman's name, just as the word *teacher* typically refers to women. In countries where male and female teachers are more equally balanced in number, further biological information is needed before we can complete the following sentence with either *him* or *her:*

> *Have you met the new teacher and how do you like _____?*

As customs change, occupational terms carry less and less information about sex—whether it is *truck driver, sea captain, doctor,* or *prime minister*.

In all the examples we have reviewed so far, there is a clear relation between sex as a biological feature and gender as a grammatical distinction: the use of *he* or *she* depends on sex. But where sex is less obvious than with adult humans, the gender system offers more choice: we may refer to a cat as either *he, she,* or *it*. With newborn animals, *it* is often used when sex is either not important or not known—even for human babies.

The gender distinction of English is suppressed entirely in the plural pronoun *they:*

> *See how he/she/it runs!*
> *See how* **they** *run!*

Although English gender correlates with sex to some extent, the tie between the grammatical category of gender and the natural feature of sex is clearly a matter of convention—of linguistic structure—rather than of nature. English speakers may use *she,* for example, to refer to cars, ships, colleges, and the like:

Just back **her** *in here!*
The Victory *lost* **her** *anchor.*

The names of countries are also frequently feminine, whether in straight prose,

France immediately recalled **her** *ambassador,*

or as Rupert Brooke's soldier thinks

   ... the thoughts by England given,
Her *sights and sounds; dreams happy as* **her** *day.*

The independence of grammatical gender from biological sex is most strikingly seen in languages like French where the two articles *le* and *la* express the distinction of masculine and feminine gender. There are hundred of cases like this:

   le *lac*   'the lake'

but

   la *rivière*   'the river'

The articles show that the word *lac* is masculine and the word *rivière* feminine but there is nothing sexual — male or female — about either lakes or rivers.

In short, the grammatical category of gender is not necessarily a logical or scientific classification of all possible entities. It is a *linguistic* category which corresponds to a greater or lesser extent to one or another natural distinction. Among the world's four thousand languages, there exists a wide variety of classification systems. It just *happens* that each language works the way it does.

Cree, as it happens, does not base its gender distinction on sex. There are separate words to refer to men and women, to be sure, just as there are separate words — in English as in Cree — for children and adults. But this is not the distinction which is reflected in grammatical gender.

Instead, Cree nouns, pronouns, and verbs fall into gender classes which correspond to the distinction, in nature, between *living* and *non-living* entities. These gender classes are called **animate** and **inanimate**. These are *grammatical* terms exactly as *masculine* and *feminine* are grammatical terms reflecting the biological classes *male* and *female*.

As one might expect, animate nouns generally refer to humans and animals (irrespective of sex, of course), but the animate class also includes words for trees and a number of frequently used household items such as pipes, kettles, or snowshoes. (If this should seem odd to speakers of English, they might think again about the gender which is assigned to the names of cars, boats, or countries.)

All other nouns are inanimate, and this class not only includes the words for objects like houses or canoes but also the terms for less palpable things such as stories or languages, or abstract nouns like "life," "leadership," or "Creeness."

How does English treat such words?

> *Leadership is an important quality but* it *is not easy to define.*

English, it turns out, not only pays attention to the sex of persons and animals but also distinguishes all of these living creatures, labelled by *he* and *she*, from everything else; the remainder is referred to by *it*. This second distinction, between masculine and feminine on the one hand and **neuter** on the other, is not all that far removed from the Cree distinction of animate and inanimate nouns.

We saw earlier that the gender of an English noun is best determined by testing which personal pronoun can be used to replace the noun: *he, she,* or *it.* We found that for some nouns, such as *Evelyn* or *teacher,* we need non-linguistic information to make that choice while there are other nouns which mark the gender by a special ending: *seamstr*ess, *lion*ess, *princ*ess, and the like. In Cree, the gender of a noun can always be determined on strictly linguistic grounds—we never need to worry about the non-linguistic world. Cree nouns have different plural endings for the two genders:

animate:
iskwēsis 'girl'	*iskwēsis*ak 'girls'
nāpēw 'man'	*nāpēw*ak 'men'
ospwākan 'pipe'	*ospwākan*ak 'pipes'

inanimate:

   astotin 'cap'   *astotin***a** 'caps'

   mōhkomān 'knife' *mōhkomān***a** 'knives'

   ācimōwin 'story'   *ācimōwin***a** 'stories'

In Cree, the gender distinction is not restricted to nouns. Different verbs are used with animate and inanimate nouns:

   niwāpamāw nāpēw   'I see a man'   (animate)

   niwāpahtēn mōhkomān   'I see a knife'   (inanimate)

   wēpinēw   'he throws him away (e.g., a pipe)'*

   wēpinam   'he throws it away'

As we shall see in chapter four, many Cree verbs come in pairs, with a special stem for each gender class; and all Cree verbs use different endings for different genders.

The shift from one gender system to another is never easy. In learning Cree, speakers of English will take a long time to remember that English *see* corresponds to two words in Cree: 'see someone' versus 'see something.' A Cree speaker learning English faces a similar problem: he has to make a distinction between *he* and *she, him* and *her, his* and *hers* in English where none is made in Cree.

For learners in either direction, mistakes are bound to be made; they are no more serious than those of a French student who says *le rivière* instead of *la rivière.* But the most typical language learning situation, probably, is for Cree-speaking children to be thrown together with English-speaking teachers — and in this difficult environment special care must be taken to keep linguistic errors in proper perspective. The Cree-speaking child who says,

   Mary combed his *hair,*

is no more stupid or "cognitively disoriented" than the English-speaking child who gets the French articles mixed up. Both are perfectly normal, pre-

---

*In this book we use *he* as a matter of convenience whenever an animate form is translated; the one pronoun *he*, therefore, refers to both males and females.

dictable mistakes which can be corrected by more practice and better teaching. Neither child needs a speech therapist or child psychologist—merely a well-trained language teacher.

Person

A third grammatical feature that English and Cree share is the category of **person**. Both languages have what might be called a "personal indexing system" which helps to sort out the participants in a conversation. In English, for example, the speaker refers to himself as *I* (first person) and he addresses *you* (second person). *We* may or may not include everyone who is listening—and it may include others out of earshot as well; *he, she,* or *they* (third person) designate still others, namely people who do not belong to the two previous categories.

The personal pronouns of English provide another example of a grammatical category which is there without being visible or audible. The number distinction is clearly expressed in the first and second person; for example, by *I* versus *we.* But it is suppressed in the second person where *you* can refer to one person or several:

	singular	plural	
first	*I*	*we*	
second	*you*		
third	*he/she/it*	*they*	

When the distinction is important, people often add something to *you: you three, you guys,* or *you all* (with or without a southern drawl).

The categories of person and number often work together in

determining the patterns of pronouns and verbs. For example, in this sentence,

> *He goes hunting every year,*

the verb *goes* is used instead of *go* in order to fit the singular- *and* third-person nature of the pronoun *he*.

The personal indexing system in Cree operates much as the English system does in the first- and second-person singular forms, since it also distinguishes between forms of *I* and *you*. But the personal pronoun forms

nīýa 'I'
kīýa 'you(sg)'

are used only when a fairly strong emphasis is intended. In verb and noun phrases they are reflected by *ni-* and *ki-*:

> ni*mōhkomān* 'my knife'
> ki*mōhkomān* 'your knife'

> ni*pimohtān* 'I walk'
> ki*pimohtān* 'you walk'

The *ni-* prefix indicates the first person singular while the *ki-* prefix marks the second person singular.

Cree makes a finer distinction than English does in the first person plural classification. The English word *we* covers several distinct groups and only the context can show which is meant:

(1) the speaker-group (*I and* _____) but not the listener-group;
(2) the speaker-group (*I or I and* _____) *and* the listener-group (*you* or *you and*__) as well.

In both cases, one or more third persons may or may not be included.

Cree is less ambiguous in this matter than English since there are two first-person forms which keep the two basic possibilities apart:

(1) the first person plural **exclusive** includes the speaker-group *but not the group being addressed:*
'*I and* _____ but not *you*';

(2)   the first person plural **inclusive** specifies that both the speaker-group *and* the hearer-group are included:
'I *(and* _____ *)* and *you (and* _____ *).*'

As an example, let us suppose that you are changing trains together with a friend. When talking to the other people who are waiting at the station, you might say things like,

We are tired from our trip,

referring to your friend and yourself. But if you continue,

Why don't we go and get some coffee?,

you obviously mean to include not just your friend but the entire group to which you are talking.* If you were speaking Cree, you could use different word forms to make this distinction clear. Notice the different prefixes and endings that reflect this distinction in the following example:

ninikamo**nān** 'we sing' (but not you) : *exclusive*
kinikamo**naw** 'we sing' (all of us, including you) : *inclusive*

Perhaps the best illustration (with apologies to all parties) is the story of the missionary who is preaching his first sermon in Cree. When he explains to his audience that *We are all sinners,* they roar with approval and laughter. Bewildered, the poor man discovers only afterwards that he had picked the wrong first person plural: instead of including his audience, he spoke only of himself and his group!

---

*Another example can be traced throughout this book. Consider two typical sentences:

(1) *We will explain this problem in more detail later.*
(2) *Let us now consider . . .*

The *we* of (1) clearly refers to the authors and does not include the readers; it is *exclusive.* The *us* of (2), on the other hand, is *inclusive:* it refers to both the authors *and* the readers.

In English, sentence (3) can be interpreted either way, but in Cree it would have to be unambiguous:

(3) *We will return to this problem later.*

Third Persons (Proximate and Obviative)

A person who neither speaks nor is spoken to is a **third person.** In Cree, the personal pronoun of the third person is *wīya*, which corresponds to English *he/she/it.* But unlike the personal pronouns of the first and second person, *wīya* is not reflected by a prefix in the corresponding verb form:

> ni*pimipahtā*n   'I run'   (first person)
> ki*pimipahtā*n   'you run'   (second person)
> *pimipahtā*w   'he runs'   (third person)

Apart from its ending, the third person verb form *pimipahtāw* is identified precisely by the absence of a personal prefix.

When there are two or more persons who are neither speakers nor listeners, the third person category may become crowded. Who does the cutting is not clear at all in the following sentence:

> *John saw Bill as he cut down a tree.*

The same ambiguity shows up in

> *Mary saw Maggie go into her house.*

Whose house? We cannot tell from the structure of the sentence.

This problem does not exist in Cree because the personal indexing system of Cree includes what has occasionally been considered a "fourth person" category. In other words, Cree has forms that can distinguish between **two** *third persons:* one that is close at hand, which is called the **proximate,** and another that is further away, called the **obviative.**

In understanding this distinction, it may be helpful to consider the dimension of **obviation** as a measure of focus: the proximate form indicates the centre of attention in a discussion—the main point of interest and often the person mentioned first—while the obviative form marks a person less important in the conversation—perhaps a figure in the background or one mentioned later. The English words *this* ("here," "now") and *that* ("further away") mark a similar contrast, but they are weak by comparison.

Proximate and obviative third persons are distinguished in Cree nouns, pronouns, and verbs:*

---

*The abbreviations (3) and (3') stand for *third person proximate* and *third person obviative;* see also the table at the end of this chapter.

> nāpēw   atimwa   wāpamēw.
> man(3)   dog(3')   see(3)
> 'The man saw the dog.'

While *nāpēw* 'man' is proximate, the noun *atimw*a 'dog' has a special obviative ending *-a*.

In the examples which follow, the main part of the sentence remains exactly as before. If we add a verb form *ē-sipwēhtē*t 'as he(3) left,' the ending *-t* agrees with the proximate noun *nāpēw* 'man(3)'; it is the man and not the dog who leaves:

> nāpēw   atimwa   wāpamēw   ē-sipwēhtēt.
> man(3)   dog(3')   see(3)   leave(3)
> 'The man saw the dog as he (the man) left.'

The verb forms *ē-sipwēhtēý*it 'as he(3') left,' on the other hand, agrees with the obviative noun *atimw*a 'dog(3')':

> nāpēw   atimwa   wāpamēw   ē-sipwēhtēýit.
> man(3)   dog(3')   see(3)   leave(3')
> 'The man saw the dog as he (the dog) left.'

Agreement between verb and noun tells us exactly who does what.

The same principle is at work in the next set of examples. The noun *cān* 'John' is proximate and *ostēs*a 'his older brother' is marked as obviative by the ending *-a:*

> cān   wāpamēw   ostēsa.
> John(3)   see(3)   his older brother(3')
> 'John saw his older brother.'

The ending *-ihk* of *wīk*ihk 'at his(3) house' indicates that the owner to whom the *his* refers is described by a proximate noun, that is, *cān:*

> cān   wāpamēw   ostēsa   wīkihk.
> John(3)   see(3)   his brother(3')   at his(3) house
> 'John saw his older brother at his (John's) house.'

The form **wīkiýihk** 'at his(3') house,' on the other hand, shows cross-reference with an obviative noun, namely *ostēsa* 'his older brother':

cān	*wāpamēw*	*ostēsa*	*wīkiýihk.*
John(3)	see(3)	his brother(3')	at his(3') house

'John saw his older brother at his (the brother's) house.'

Only one person is proximate at any one time. If there are more than two third persons, therefore, we may end up with two or more obviative nouns. In that case, other cues (such as context, stress, and word order) must be used to keep the various persons apart.

Another way to solve this problem is to reassign the rôles. The noun *atimw*a 'dog(s),' for example, is obviative in sentence (a) and again in (c); in (b), however, the dogs are given the central rôle and the noun *atimw*ak 'dogs' is proximate:

(a) *nāpēw*   *nīso*   *atimwa*   *wāpamēw.*
     man(3)   two   dog(3')   see(3)
     'The man saw two dogs.'

(b) *atimwak*   *ē-pimipahtācik.*
     dog(3p)   run(3p)
     'The dogs were running.'

(c) *ēkwa*   *nāpēw*   *atimwa*   *ē-pimitisahwāt.*
     then   man(3)   dog(3')   follow(3)
     'Then the man chased the dogs.'

The present example is necessarily somewhat simplified, but the texts of chapter six contain a number of authentic instances of focus shifts.

As nouns and verbs change from proximate to obviative and back to proximate, they respond to the limitations of the grammatical machinery. But they also reflect changes in the topic of a discussion or, when a story is told, the shifts in focus which move the actors on and off the stage.

Direction

In addition to gender, number, and person there is a fourth major grammatical category in Cree: **direction** concerns the relationship in a sentence between the **actor** and the **goal**. As in earlier sections of this chapter, an illustration from English may help to make this idea clear by showing the differences between Cree and English.

Consider these two sentences:

> (1a) *The cat* is *scratch*ing *the girl.*
> (1b) *The girl* is **being** *scratch*ed **by** *the cat.*

They are very different in the verb forms they use, in word order, and even in their grammatical subjects: in (1a) *the cat* is the subject; in (1b) it is *the girl*. If we consider what really happened, on the other hand, it turns out that both sentences describe the same event: the cat did the scratching and the girl ended up with the scratches. The grammatical function of *the girl* as object in (1a) and as subject in (1b) obviously has little bearing on her getting scratched. The primary difference between active and passive sentences in English is one of emphasis and style: the actor-goal relationship (who acts, and who is at the receiving end of the action) is not affected by it.*

In Cree as well as in English, differences in emphasis can be expressed in a variety of ways, including word-order changes, special intonations, special sentence types (*It is the girl who was scratched by the cat*) etc.

---

*The fact that certain verb phrases seem to be reversible is merely a red herring:

> (a) *I saw John.*
> (b) *I was seen by John.*

For if we consider (b) more closely, it is not the passive of (a) but of another sentence, (c):

> (c) *John saw me.*

The passive of (a), then, is *not* (b) but a fourth sentence, (d):

> (d) *John was seen by me.*

However, the *direction* category of Cree is very different indeed, in spite of some partial resemblance (which has led to a great deal of confusion in writings about Cree). Direction is not a matter of emphasis; instead, it has to do with the actor-goal relationship, as in these verbs:

(2a) *niwāpamāw atim.* 'I see the dog.'
  see(1–3)   dog (3)

(2b) *niwāpamik atim.* 'The dog sees me.'
  see(3–1)   dog(3)

Probably the most striking thing about these two sentences is the *lack* of a striking difference: both only have two words and in the same order; the only differences are two sounds at the end of the verb, *-āw : -ik*. These two sounds, which comprise merely a small part of each word, make exactly the same difference as a complete change-around of words in English:

(1a) *The* cat *is scratching the* girl.
(1c) *The* girl *is scratching the* cat.

English has very strict rules of word order; as the last example shows, word order makes a lot of difference. In Cree, by contrast, word order is primarily a matter of style and emphasis. It does not help much in clarifying the relationship between the actor and the goal since in Cree sentences word order is fairly free. Yet, as we have seen, there are other signs to reveal the relationship, for the verb shows *by its form* which is which.

All verbs which involve both actor and goal (transitive animate verbs, see chapter four) include a special *direction marker* for this purpose. Although all the other parts of the verb may be exactly the same, indicating, for example, that a first person plural exclusive (*ni- -nān-*) and a proximate third person plural (*-ak*) are involved, it is the direction markers *-ā-* and *-iko-* which make the difference between

(4a) *niwī-nipahānānak   nīso   mōswak.*
  want-to-kill(1p–3p)   two   moose(3p)
  'We wanted to kill two moose.'

and   (4b) *niwī-nipahikonānak nīso   mōswak.*
          want-to-kill(3p–ip)   two   moose(3p)
          'Two moose wanted to kill us.'

The situation we have discussed so far is the *basic type of direction* which is crucial to an understanding of Cree structure. Before going on to a somewhat more complex type, it is worth remembering that this Cree category of direction has little in common with the English distinction of active and passive. Whether we actually translate this sentence,

(5) *kimiskawāw   nitōspwākan.*
     find(2–3)   my pipe (3)

as 'You found my pipe' or as 'My pipe was found by you' is of no relevance at all to Cree; it is strictly a matter of English style.

A much more complex type of direction occurs where a verb involves two third persons; in such a situation, *obviation* (which is a matter of focus, see page 25) plays an important rôle. In the simplest case of actor-goal reversal,* the verb is left unchanged and the reversal is accomplished by switching the noun endings:

(6a) *wāpamēw   nāpēw   sīsīpa.*
      see(3)   man(3)   duck(3')
      'The man sees the duck.'

---

*In the most complex case, the verb indicates the direction but, since the previous sentence may require a particular obviation arrangement, things are liable to get tricky:

(6c) *wāpamik   nāpēw   sīsīpa.*
      see(3')   man(3)   duck(3')
      'The duck sees the man.'

(6d) *wāpamik   nāpēwa   sīsīp.*
      see(3')   man(3')   duck(3)
      'The man sees the duck.'

In other words, (6a) means exactly the same as (6d), and (6b) means exactly the same as (6c); their only difference is one of different environments, and possibly of style.

(6b) *wāpamēw   nāpēwa   sīsīp.*
      see(3)   man(3') duck(3)
      'The duck sees the man.'

This is very similar to our English examples (1a) and (1c) but with one difference: in English the reversal requires a change in word order whereas in Cree the endings suffice to indicate who is the actor and who is the goal. The verb ending *-ēw* shows that a proximate third person (3) is acting upon an obviative one (3'), and the ending *-a* identifies 'duck' in (6a) and 'man' in (6b) as the obviative and, consequently, the goal.

One concluding note here on the changing forms of verbs concerns those verbs that are used as commands. Cree as well as English has command forms for making orders like *Listen to me* or *Give it to your father*. In Cree these forms change according to whether the receiver of the action is first person or third person. Notice in the examples below that different endings are used to distinguish between action toward 'me' and action toward 'him':

     pēhik   'wait for me!'
     pēhihk   'wait for him!'

If the various distinctions drawn in this chapter seem quite abstract and difficult to grasp, remember that they have been discussed only briefly and with mere passing reference to their actual use in the construction of Cree words and sentences. Without the grammatical categories that we have surveyed, words would stand in isolation rather than being joined into phrases and sentences. But the fundamental classifications of gender, number, person, and direction also play a *rôle* in the make-up of individual words. In chapters three and four we will examine the way in which these underlying patterns are reflected in the surface shape of Cree words.

The Personal Indexing System of Cree:
Summary and Abbreviations

Gender	Person	Obviation	Number	Code
animate	indefinite		sg/pl	indf
	first (inclusive)		pl	21
	first		sg	1
	(exclusive)		pl	1p
	second		sg	2
			pl	2p
	third	proximate	sg	3
			pl	3p
		obviative	sg/pl	3'
inanimate		proximate	sg	0
			pl	0p
		obviative	sg	0'
			pl	0'p

3 The Shape of Words: Noun Inflection

What is a word?

The question seems simple enough, and yet we might have some difficulty in deciding whether *dog* and *dogs*, for example, are one word or two.

As we look at them or listen to them, the evidence seems clear: *dog* is not the same as *dogs*; therefore, they are two words. This conclusion seems reasonable if we consider further that the word *dog* has something in common with the words *cat, tree, child* which it does not share with the words *dogs, cats, trees, children*. The two sets of words are distinguished by the category of number that we discussed in the previous chapter: the first is *singular*, the second *plural*.

Viewed from another perspective, however, *dog* and *dogs* are obviously the same word: except for the last sound of *dogs*, they consist of the same sequence of sounds and they have the same meaning—except for the difference in number.

The dilemma leads us to recognize that *dog* and *dogs* are different versions of the same element. Words can take on different forms, from *dog* : *dogs* to *child* : *children* and *goose* : *geese*. Even greater discrepancies in shape are found in English verbs, from *dance* : *danced* and *sing* : *sang* to *teach* : *taught* and the extreme case of *go* : *went*.

The varying **forms** of a word carry information beyond the meaning of the **stem**. As a plural form, *dogs* defines not only the kind of animal but also tells us that there are at least two. The form *dog*, which looks so simple, is not merely the stem either: it does double duty because in addition to signalling "a certain four-legged animal" (or the like) it also means: "and there is only *one* of them."

As words appear in various inflected forms, they express the grammatical categories which were introduced in chapter two: number, gender, person, and direction.

Although both Cree and English use inflected forms to distinguish, say, singular from plural, inflection is of far greater importance in Cree. The grammatical category of direction provides a clear example. English relies almost entirely on word order to signal who does what to whom. In Cree, the same relations are expressed by inflectional elements which appear at the beginning or end of a word.

These inflectional elements may follow the stem:

> *mōhkomān*   'knife'
> *mōhkomān*a   'knives'

or they may precede it:

> ni*mōhkomān*   'my knife'
> ki*mōhkomān*   'your(sg) knife'

But the stem may also be surrounded by these inflectional elements:

> ni*mōhkomān*a   'my knives'

The elements which come before the stem, like *ni-*, are called **prefixes** and those like *-a*, which are placed *after* the stem, **suffixes**.

In the previous examples, the prefix *ni-* means 'my' and the suffix *-a* expresses the plural status of the noun 'knife': 'knives.' While 'my' is signalled by the prefix *ni-* alone, it takes both a prefix *and* a suffix to express 'our':

> ni*mōhkomān*inān   'our(excl) knife'

This prefix-suffix combination may, in turn, be followed by the plural suffix *-a:*

nimōhkomānināna   'our(excl) knives'

This last form, then, ends in two inflectional suffixes (*-inān* and *-a*) which follow one another.

In a noun form like *nimōhkomānināna*, we may think of the inflectional elements as being arranged in two layers which can be peeled off like the skins of an onion. Prefixes like *ni-* 'I, my' and prefix-suffix combinations like *ni- -inān* 'we(excl), our(excl)' belong to the **inner** layer. The status of the noun with respect to number, gender, and obviation is indicated by the suffixes of the **outer** layer.

The Outer Layer: Number and Obviation

The grammatical categories which were introduced in chapter two rarely occur by themselves. The plural endings (or the lack of one) express the category of *number;* but, at the same time, the particular plural ending which is used (*-ak* or *-a*) also reveals the *gender* of the noun: animate or inanimate.

In either gender, the (proximate) singular is indicated by the *lack* of a special ending. In this respect, Cree and English are very much alike: in both languages, the singular (that is, the proximate singular in the case of Cree animate nouns) is the simplest form of the noun:

> *sīsīp : duck*
> *mīnis : berry*

A special suffix is added to form the plural:

> *sīsīpak : ducks*
> *mīnisa : berries*

In both languages, therefore, the (proximate) singular form can be treated as the noun **stem**.*

The distinction between the two third persons is made differently for animate and inanimate nouns. Inanimate nouns do not have inflectional endings** to distinguish the *proximate* (central, in focus) from the *obviative* (further away, background). For animate nouns, on the other hand, there is a clear distinction, made by inflectional elements, between proximate and obviative. The obviative form, in turn, does not keep apart singular and plural.

The endings which signal number (*sg* or *pl*) and obviation (*prox* or *obv*) are as follows; the symbol **Ø** 'zero' stands for nothing at all.

---

*While this approach is the most practical one for the present purpose, a different analysis is preferred in a more technical context.

**Although they do not use an obviative suffix, the obviation status (proximate or obviative) of inanimate nouns is reflected in the corresponding verbs; *ē-misāk* is proximate, *ē-misāýik* is obviative:

> niwāpahtēn   mōhkomān   ē-misāk.
> see(1)   knife   be-big(0)
> 'I saw a knife which was big(prox).'

> wāpahtam   mōhkomān   ē-misāýik.
> see(3)   knife   be-big(0')
> 'He(prox) saw a knife which was big(obv).'

In the eastern half of the Cree-speaking area, special obviative endings may occur with inanimate nouns. The second of the above Plains Cree sentences, for example, would be

> wāpahtam   mōhkomāniniw   ē-misānik.
> see(3)   knife(0')   be-big(0')
> 'He(prox) saw a knife(obv) which was big(obv).'

in the eastern variety of Swampy Cree.

Animate nouns:

-Ø	prox **sg**	*sīsīp* 'duck'
-ak	prox **pl**	*sīsīpak* 'ducks'
-a	**obv** sg/pl	*sīsīpa* 'duck' *or* 'ducks'

Inanimate nouns:

-Ø	prox/obv **sg**	*mīnis* 'berry'
-a	prox/obv **pl**	*mīnisa* 'berries'

In the abbreviations of the number and obviation categories, the most important feature is set in **boldface** letters.

The diagrams which follow show the interplay of the grammatical categories and the relations among the endings which express them:

ANIMATE:

	OBVIATION				OBVIATION	
	prox	obv			prox	obv
NUMBER sg	*-Ø*			**NUMBER** sg	*sīsīp*	
		-a				*sīsīpa*
pl	*-ak*			pl	*sīsīpak*	

INANIMATE:

	OBVIATION			OBVIATION	
	prox	obv		prox	obv
NUMBER sg	*-Ø*		**NUMBER** sg	*mīnis*	
pl	*-a*		pl	*mīnisa*	

Stem Types

The stems *sīsip-* and *mīnis-* represent the most common type of noun stems.* The vast majority of Cree nouns, whether animate or inanimate, belong to this stem type, which we call *Type I*. The other types, which are much less common, differ from *Type I* nouns in the shape of the stem.

The nouns of *Type II* end in *a* or *i*, as *niska* 'goose' or *wāwi* 'egg'; all forms of these nouns consist of two syllables.

With animate nouns like *niska*, the final *-a* disappears and *-ak* is added to the stem for the proximate plural form, while *nothing* is added for the obviative. In other words, animate *Type II* nouns have the same form in the proximate singular and the obviative:

niska	'goose'	prox sg
niskak	'geese'	prox pl
niska	'goose' or 'geese'	obv sg/pl

The singular form of inanimate *Type II* nouns ends in *-i*, which is replaced by *-a* in the plural:

wāwi	'egg'	prox/obv sg
wāwa	'eggs'	prox/obv pl

Type III nouns have a proximate singular form ending in one of the four consonants *k*, *m*, *n*, or *s*. In all other forms of *Type III* nouns, a *w* appears between these consonants and the endings:

---

*When writing stems, we always put a hyphen at the end; this practice reduces confusion between the singular form *sīsip*, which is opposed to the plural form *sīsipak*, and the stem *sīsip-*, which is common to both of them.

atim 'dog'	prox sg (animate)
*atim*wak 'dogs'	prox pl
*atim*wa 'dog' *or* 'dogs'	obv sg/pl

| *maskēk* 'swamp' | prox/obv sg (inanimate) |
| *maskēk*wa 'swamps' | prox/obv pl |

The nouns of *Type IV* end in a sequence of a vowel and either of the semivowels *y* or *w*. They behave exactly like the nouns of *Type I* when the plural endings and the like are added:

| *mīnisāpoy* 'berry broth' | prox/obv sg (inanimate) |
| *mīnisāpoya* 'berry broths' | prox/obv pl |

With a suffix beginning in *i*, however, a different pattern occurs; the *yi* or *wi* sequence disappears and the vowel which precedes it is lengthened.* With the place-suffix *-ihk*, for example, which is presented in the next section, we find this form:

(*mīnisāpoy+ihk*)
mīnisāpōhk 'in the berry broth'

The chart which follows summarizes the nouns we have discussed in this section and their inflection for number and obviation.

		I (and IV)		II		III	
animate	prox sg	*sīsip*	'duck'	*nisk*a	'goose'	*atim*	'dog'
	pl	*sīsip*ak	'ducks'	*nisk*ak	'geese'	*atim*wak	'dogs'
	obv	*sīsip*a	'duck' or 'ducks'	*nisk*a	'goose' or 'geese'	*atim*wa	'dog' or 'dogs'
inanimate	sg	*minis*	'berry'	*wāwi*	'egg'	*maskēk*	'swamp'
	pl	*minisa*	'berries'	*wāwa*	'eggs'	*maskēk*wa	'swamps'

*This is vowel adjustment rule 1; see also the summary at the end of this chapter.

Place-forms

Nouns also have a **locative** ending which is used to indicate place or position. The place-forms of Cree nouns are words which correspond to such prepositional phrases of English as "in the house" or "at the lake." The locative suffix is *-ihk*:

ospwākan 'pipe'	prox sg (animate)
ospwākanihk 'in a pipe'	loc

sākahikan 'lake'	prox/obv sg (inanimate)
sākahikanihk 'in, on, *or* at a lake'	loc

ospwākan- and *sākahikan-* are noun stems of *Type I*.

In *Type II* nouns, the final vowel disappears before the locative ending is added:

kōna 'snow'	prox sg (animate)
(*kōn+ihk*)	
kōnihk 'in the snow'	loc

Type III nouns introduce us to another kind of vowel adjustment.* When the stem with its final *w* is followed by the locative suffix with its initial *i*, then *w* and *i* merge, yielding *o*:

maskēk 'swamp'	prox/obv sg (inanimate)
maskēkwa 'swamps'	prox/obv pl
(*maskēkw+ihk*)	
maskēkohk 'in a swamp'	loc

---

*This is vowel adjustment rule 2; see also the summary at the end of this chapter.

Type IV nouns in the locative provide many examples of vowel adjustment rule 1:

ōtēnaw 'town'	prox/obv sg (inanimate)
(*ōtēnaw+ihk*)	
ōtēnāhk 'in town'	loc
watay 'his belly'	prox/obv sg (inanimate)
(*watay+ihk*)	
watāhk 'in *or* on his belly'	loc

When a noun stem is followed by the locative ending, it cannot at the same time take any of the endings which indicate number and obviation.

Address-forms

The **vocative**, or address-form, is another noun form of Cree which has no parallel in English. It is used to address someone directly. Cree speakers use one form to call out to someone:

nōhkō '(my) grandmother!'

and another when speaking about the same person (as in "My grandmother lives over there"):

nōhkom 'my grandmother'

Vocatives are most commonly used to address family members. Among the younger generation of Cree speakers, the use of the special address-forms seems to be declining.

There is also a vocative plural form, to be used in addressing several people:

nōhkomitik '(my) grandmothers!'

This form is based on the suffix *-itik* which is added to the normal stem.

The singular address-form *nōhkō* differs from all the other forms of the stem *nōhkom-;* the final consonant is lost and the vowel which now ends the word is lengthened:

nōhkō	'(my) grandmother!'	voc sg
nōhkomitik	'(my) grandmothers!'	voc pl

nōhkom	'my grandmother'	prox sg (animate)
nōhkomak	'my grandmothers'	prox pl
nōhkoma	'my grandmother(s)'	obv sg/pl

The same pattern of forming the vocative singular is found with several further stems, but in another common formation the suffix *-ē* is added to the stem in its normal form:

nistēsē	'(my) older brother!'	voc sg
nistēsitik	'(my) older brothers!'	voc pl

nistēs	'my older brother'	prox sg (animate)
nistēsak	'my older brothers'	prox pl
nistēsa	'my older brother(s)'	obv sg/pl

The vocative form *nistēsē* and its counterpart *nisīmitik* '(my) little brothers!' occur a number of times in the conversation of text A in chapter six.

The Inner Layer: Possession

The rôle of a noun within the sentence (and sometimes beyond) is defined by inflection. The suffixes of the *outer* layer express the relations between nouns and verbs: either by agreement in number, gender, and obviation or in the more specialized functions of place-form and address-forms.

The inflectional patterns of the *inner* layer relate one noun to another. In

   cān omōhkomān   'John's knife,'

for example, the *o-* of *omōhkomān* 'his knife' refers back to *cān* 'John.' The noun may also refer back to a first or second person which is expressed by the pronominal prefixes *ni-* 'I, my' or *ki-* 'you(sg), your(sg)':

> *nimōhkomān*   'my knife'
> *kimōhkomān*   'your(sg) knife'

The independent pronouns *nīýa* 'I,' *kīýa* 'you(sg)' etc., are used only for emphasis.

Nouns with the personal prefixes *ni-*, *ki-*, and *o-* indicate **cross-reference** or **possession**. Although the latter term is convenient (not least, perhaps, because it recalls the *possessive* pronouns of English), it must not be taken too literally. You may actually own *your knife* or some other piece of property; but in *my grandfather* the relation is one of belonging rather than of ownership—and the cross-reference may be much more abstract yet, as in *his age* or *his being from Alberta has nothing to do with it*. In short, cross-reference or possession is another *grammatical* category.

In English, the grammatical category of possession is expressed in two ways. For full nouns, the noun to which reference is made has a special ending which we normally write with an *s* and an apostrophe:

> *John's hat*
> *my mother's health*
> *the teachers' competence*

When there is no need to repeat the full noun, we can use pronouns instead:

> *his hat*
> *her health*
> *their competence*

For first and second persons as well, the possessive pronouns of English are separate words:

> *my health*   *our health*
> *your(sg) health*   *your(pl) health*

Cree, as we have seen, uses a prefix instead:

ni- 'I, my'	ni*maskisin* 'my shoe'
ki- 'you(sg), your(sg)'	ki*maskisin* 'your(sg) shoe'
o- 'his'	o*maskisin* 'his shoe'

If the stem begins in a vowel, as *astotin-* 'cap,' the personal prefixes end in a connective *t*:

nit*astotin*	'my cap'
kit*astotin*	'your(sg) cap'
ot*astotin*	'his cap'

The possessors that we have illustrated so far were all singular: 'I,' 'you,' 'he.' For the plural possessors 'we(excl),' 'we(incl),' 'you,' and 'they,' Cree uses personal suffixes in addition to the personal prefixes:

ni*maskisin*inān	'our(excl) shoe'
ki*maskisin*inaw	'our(incl) shoe'
ki*maskisin*iwāw	'your(pl) shoe'
o*maskisin*iwāw	'their shoe'

In these forms, the inner layer of inflection completely surrounds the stem.

The prefixes and suffixes of the inner layer of noun inflection are summarized below. The forms for third person possessors are discussed in a later section.

ni(t)-	1	'my'
ki(t)-	2	'your(sg)'
o(t)-	3	'his(prox)'
o(t)- -iẏiw	3'	'his(obv)'
ni(t)- -inān	1p	'our(excl)'
ki(t)- -inaw	21	'our(incl)'
ki(t)- -iwāw	2p	'your(pl)'
o(t)- -iwāw	3p	'their'

In *Type II* nouns, the final vowel is dropped before the suffixes are added:

    mihti 'firewood'   prox/obv sg (inanimate)
    (ki+miht+inaw)
    kimihtinaw 'our (incl) firewood'

The final *w* of *Type III* nouns merges with the initial *i* of the suffixes to yield *o:**

    (ki+skīsikw+iwāw+a)
    kiskīsikowāwa 'your (pl) eyes'   prox/obv pl (inanimate)

In *Type IV* nouns, the sequence of stem-final *y* or *w* and suffix-initial *i* disappears and the preceding vowel is lengthened:**

    mēskanaw 'road'   prox/obv sg (inanimate)
    (o+mēskanaw+iwāw)
    omēskanāwāw 'their road'

Dependent Stems

Any Cree noun may take the inflectional elements of the inner layer. Some nouns form a special possession stem before the prefixes and suffixes of the inner layer can be attached. This form of the stem is based on an element *-im-* which is suffixed directly to the normal stem:

    sīsīp 'duck'   prox sg (animate)
    nisīsīpim 'my duck'
    nisīsīpimak 'my ducks'
    nisīsīpiminān 'our (excl) duck'
    nisīsīpiminānak 'our (excl) ducks'
etc.

---

*This is vowel adjustment rule 2; see also the summary at the end of this chapter.

**This is vowel adjustment rule 1; see also the summary at the end of this chapter.

In nouns of *Type III*, the *i* of *-im-* merges with stem-final *w* to yield *o:**

> *mistik* 'stick'   prox/obv sg (inanimate)
> *mistikwa* 'sticks'
> *(ni+mistik*w+*im+a)*
> *nimistikoma* 'my sticks'

In *Type IV* nouns, the sequence of stem-final *y* or *w* and suffix-initial *i* disappears and the preceding vowel is lengthened (if it is not already long, as in our example):**

> *nāpēw* 'man'   prox sg (animate)
> *(ni+nāpēw+im)*
> *nināpēm* 'my man, husband'

There is one group of nouns which must *always* be inflected for possession. These are called **dependent** nouns (and all others may thus be called *independent*). Dependent nouns refer to body-parts, relatives, and a few important personal possessions; for example:

> **ni***skīsik* 'my eye'
> **n***atay* 'my belly'
> **ni***mosōm* 'my grandfather'
> **nō***hkom* 'my grandmother'
> **ni***tēm* 'my dog *or* horse'
> **nī***ki* 'my home'

Several of these examples show another peculiarity of dependent stems: they often take the personal prefixes without the vowel *i*; that is, they have *n-* or *k-* instead of *ni(t)-* or *ki(t)-*. In the third person, the prefix *o(t)-* then takes the form *w-* (except before *o* or *ō* where it disappears altogether):

---

*This is vowel adjustment rule 2; see also the summary at the end of this chapter.

**This is vowel adjustment rule 1; see also the summary at the end of this chapter.

w*atay*   'his belly'
ō*hkoma*   'his grandmother' (animate, with obviative ending)
w*īki*   'his home' (inanimate, no obviative ending)

If one wants to use these nouns without specifying a particular possessor, there is a general possessor prefix *mi-*. This prefix indicates a noun which has no cross-reference to anyone:

> **mi***skīsik*   'an eye'

Note also the use of *misit* as the measure 'foot':

> **ni***sit*   'my foot'
> **mi***sit*   'a foot'

The dependent stem *-tēm-* 'dog *or* horse' does not have a form for general possessor; instead, it is paralleled by the independent noun *atim*. The noun *atim*, in turn, does not take the inflectional elements of the inner layer.

Combining Both Layers: Third Person Possessors

With most nouns, there is no special ending to show that they are in the (proximate) singular. In the plural, however, when endings like *-ak* or *-a* are added, two layers of inflection are visibly present in the same form. In the examples which follow, the inanimate plural ending *-a* belongs to the outer layer while the possession prefixes and suffixes *ni-* and *-inān* belong to the inner layer:

> **ni***maskisin*a   'my shoes'
> **ni***maskinin*ān*a   'our (excl) shoes'

The locative ending *-ihk*, which is part of the outer layer, may similarly be added to the inflections of the inner layer:

> ni*maskisin*ihk   'in *or* on my shoe'
> ni*maskisin*inānihk   'in *or* on our(excl) shoe'

In the examples of this section, we use boldface letters for the inflectional elements of the inner layer and plain Roman type for those of the outer layer.

In our earlier discussion of the inner layer we had used the stems *maskisin-* 'shoe' and *astotin-* 'cap' as our major examples. Since these two stems are inanimate, we did not need to be concerned (in the western Cree dialects, at least) with the inflectional distinction of proximate and obviative.

If an animate noun, however, is inflected for possession, close attention must be paid to the distinction of proximate and obviative as soon as there are two persons. With the animate stem *asām-* 'snowshoe,' for example, we find

> **ni***asām*   'my snowshoe'
> **ki***asām*   'your snowshoe'

but

> **o***asām*a   'his snowshoe(s)'

The noun refers back to a third person 'he' to whom the snowshoe belongs, and that third person is proximate (in focus). As a consequence, the word for snowshoe is obviative (less central), as shown by the ending *-a*.

The proximate possessor may, of course, also be expressed by a noun, as in

niwāpamāw	*nāpēw*	*o*tasāma	*ē-osīhāt.*
see(1–3)	man(3)	his(3) snowshoes(3')	make(3)

'I saw a man(prox) preparing his(prox) snowshoes(obv).'

But what if the possessor of the snowshoes is already obviative? In the next sentence, *cān* 'John' is proximate and *nāpēwa* 'man' is obviative. The verb *ē-osīhāýit* 'as he(3') prepares him' agrees with *nāpēwa* and is also obviative. And the inflections of the inner layer include a special prefix-suffix combination to show that the snowshoes belong to the obviative noun *nāpēwa* 'man' rather than to the proximate noun *cān* 'John':*

> *wāpamēw*   *cān*   *nāpēwa*   *otasāmiẏiwa*   *ē-osīhāẏit.*
> see(3)   John(3)   man(3′)   his(3′) snowshoes(3′)   make(3′)
> 'John(prox) saw a man(obv) preparing(obv) his(obv)
>   snowshoes(obv).'

For an obviative possessor, then, the inner layer of inflection completely surrounds the stem: the prefix *o-* is combined with the suffix *-iẏiw*. In the case of animate nouns, this inner-layer suffix *-iẏiw* is followed by the outer-layer suffix *-a* which marks the obviative status of the noun itself:

> **ot*asāmi*ẏiwa**   'the other's(*obv*) snowshoe(obv)'

Compare the form for a proximate possessor:

> **ot*asām*a**   'his(*prox*) snowshoe(obv)'

For inanimate nouns, the contrast between proximate and obviative possessors is expressed by the same combination of the prefix *o-* and the suffix *-iẏiw*, but there is no obviative ending of the outer layer:

> **om*askisini*ẏiw**   'the other's(*obv*) shoe'

as compared with the form for a proximate possessor:

> **om*askisin***   'his(*prox*) shoe'

The suffix *-a* which may end these forms makes them look exactly like the forms of animate nouns, but it has a completely different function. With inanimate nouns, *-a* is the suffix which marks the plural:

---

*This sentence, incidentally, illustrates the concluding remarks of our discussion of obviation in chapter two: there are *two* obviative nouns which agree with the verb *ē-osīhāẏit*. Aside from word order, it is our knowledge of the external circumstances which suggests that the man prepares his snowshoes and not the other way around.

omaskisiniýiwa   'the other's(obv) shoes'
omaskisina   'his(prox) shoes'

With a third person possessor, the interplay of the two layers of inflection can become quite complex. The chart displays the possible combinations of inflectional elements.

The inflectional elements in the case of a third person possessor

	INNER LAYER: *Possession*		OUTER LAYER: *Number and Obviation*
Prefix		Suffix	Suffix
			ANIMATE
o- 'third person'	STEM	*-Ø* 'prox sg' *-iwāw* 'prox pl' *-iýiw* 'obv sg/pl'	*-a* 'obv sg/pl'
			INANIMATE
			-Ø '(obv) sg' *-a* '(obv) pl'

(Note: The symbol Ø stands for nothing at all.)

The tables which follow show the most common combinations of the two layers of inflection: **possession** and **number-obviation.***

---

*The abbreviations of the gender-number-person-obviation categories are defined in the table at the end of chapter two.

Inanimate Noun

Stem *maskisin-* 'shoe':

Possession

	prox/obv **sg**	prox/obv **pl**	
I	*nimaskisin*	*nimaskisina*	'my shoe, shoes'
2	*kimaskisin*	*kimaskisina*	'your (sg) shoe, shoes'
3	*omaskisin*	*omaskisina*	'his (prox) shoe, shoes'
3'	*omaskisiniýiw*	*omaskisiniýiwa*	'his (obv) shoe, shoes'
ip	*nimaskisininān*	*nimaskisinināna*	'our (excl) shoe, shoes'
2I	*kimaskisininaw*	*kimaskisininawa*	'our (incl) shoe, shoes'
2p	*kimaskisiniwāw*	*kimaskisiniwāwa*	'your (pl) shoe, shoes'
3p	*omaskisiniwāw*	*omaskisiniwāwa*	'their shoe, shoes'

Animate Noun

Dependent stem *-tēm-* 'horse, dog':

Possession

	prox **sg**	prox **pl**	obv sg/pl	
I	*nitēm*	*nitēmak*	*nitēma*	'my horse' (etc.)
2	*kitēm*	*kitēmak*	*kitēma*	'your (sg) horse'
3			*otēma*	'his (prox) horse'
3'			*otēmiýiwa*	'his (obv) horse'
ip	*nitēminān*	*nitēminānak*	*nitēmināna*	'our (excl) horse' (etc.)
2I	*kitēminaw*	*kitēminawak*	*kitēminawa*	'our (incl) horse'
2p	*kitēmiwāw*	*kitēmiwāwak*	*kitēmiwāwa*	'your (pl) horse'
3p			*otēmiwāwa*	'their horse'

Pronoun Inflection

There are a few pronouns, like *kotak* 'another,' which use the same endings as the outer layer of noun inflection. But the most common pronouns of Cree, such as *awa* 'this' and *ana* 'that,' use a different set of endings to show the same distinctions:

animate						
	prox	sg	*kotak*	*awa*	*ana*
		pl	*kotakak*	*ōki*	*aniki*
	obv		*kotaka*	*ōhi*	*anihi*
inanimate		sg	*kotak*	*ōma*	*anima*
		pl	*kotaka*	*ōhi*	*anihi*

Summary of Vowel Adjustment Rules

Vowel adjustment rule 1:

If an inflectional element which ends in the sequence **vowel + semivowel** (*w* or *y*) is followed by a suffix beginning in **i**, the semivowel and the *i* disappear and the vowel is lengthened if it is not already long:

$$\left. \begin{array}{l} V\ w + i \\ V\ y + i \end{array} \right\} \longrightarrow \bar{V}$$

Vowel adjustment rule 2:

If a stem which ends in the sequence **consonant + w** is followed by a suffix beginning in **i**, the *w* and the *i* merge, yielding *o*:

$$C\ w + i \longrightarrow C\ o$$

Examples may be found throughout this chapter; for further instances see the texts of chapter six.

The Shape of Words:
Verb Inflection

Cree verbs have much in common with Cree nouns. Verbs appear in more varied forms than nouns but they express the same grammatical categories: *number, gender,* and *person,* with the last including the distinction of *proximate* and *obviative.* Verbs which include inflectional elements for two persons rely on the further category of *direction* to signal which is the actor and which the goal.

The shared grammatical categories are the most fundamental parallel between the verbs and nouns of Cree, but they are not the only one. All verbs, for instance, have forms which use both prefixes and suffixes to signal the grammatical categories: the stem is surrounded, as we saw in the case of nouns, by layers of inflectional elements which resemble the skins of an onion. In

     ni*pēhā*nānak,

for example, you may recognize the prefix-suffix combination *ni- -nān* 'we(excl), our(excl)' and the animate plural suffix *-ak.* In a noun like

     ni*tēmi*nānak   'our(excl) horses'

these same* prefixes and suffixes are used to mark the possessor ('we, our') and the number status of the noun itself ('two or more horses'). In the verb form

     ni*pēhā*nānak   'we(excl) wait for them'

---

*The differences in form are generally slight: the first person plural exclusive suffix is *-inān* with a noun stem and *-nān* with verb stems. This variation is similar to that found with

they indicate the two persons which are signalled by this form: the prefix-suffix combination *ni- -nān* 'we (excl)' marks the actor, and the goal 'them' is defined by the plural suffix *-ak*.

While expressing the same grammatical categories, these inflectional endings refer to slightly different entities: in the case of *nitēminānak* they refer to possessor and noun; in the verb *nipēhānānak* they refer to the two person *rôles*, actor and goal. Yet the verb and noun forms are remarkably parallel not only in the inflectional endings they use but in the way these are arranged into the familiar structure of outer and inner layers. In this sentence,

> ni*tēmi*nānak ni*pēhā*nānak.
> 'We (excl) were waiting for our (excl) horses.'

you have to look very carefully (or, of course, know the stems) to tell which is the noun and which is the verb.

For verbs as for nouns, Cree places much more weight on the *shape* of the word than on its position in the sentence.

---

different noun stems:

    *nimaskisin*ināna   'our (excl) shoes'

but

    *nimēskan*ānāna   'our (excl) roads'

For the most part, such differences reflect the vowel and consonant adjustments between adjoining inflectional elements (see the summary of vowel adjustment rules at the end of chapter three).

With nouns and verbs alike, the personal prefixes end in a connective *t* if the stem begins in a vowel:

    ni*tasāmi*nānak   'our (excl) snowshoes'
    ni*tasamā*nānak   'we (excl) feed them'

Agreement

There are, of course, also many differences between the nouns and verbs of Cree. The grammatical category of gender, for example plays a major rôle in both—but in different ways and by different means.

Nouns have gender, verbs merely express it: the gender expressed by a Cree verb is that of the noun which functions either as actor or as goal. Verbs which agree with an *actor* noun only (or *intransitive* verbs) express the gender of that noun:*

> *ospwākan*ak   *mihcētiw*ak.
> pipe(3p)   be-numerous(3p)
> 'There were many pipes(animate).'

> *mōhkomān*a   *mihcētinw*a.
> knife(0p)   be-numerous(0p)
> 'There were many knives(inanimate).'

Verbs which agree with both an *actor* **and** a *goal* (or *transitive* verbs) express the gender of the goal noun:

> *niwēpinā*w   *ospwākan.*
> throw(1–3)   pipe(3)
> 'I threw the pipe(animate) away.'

> *niwēpinē*n   *mōhkomān.*
> throw(1–0)   knife(0)
> 'I threw the knife(inanimate) away.'

While the (proximate) singular forms *ospwākan* and *mōhkomān* show no external evidence of gender, they are used with different verb forms.

In the above examples, the inherent gender of the nouns and the gender that verbs express on behalf of their actors and goals are indicated in a

---

*The abbreviations of the gender-number-person-obviation categories are defined in the table at the end of chapter two.

similar way. The stems themselves do not signal gender but the endings differ according to the gender of the stem. To test for gender, then, we need only form the plural of a noun:*

> *ospwākan*ak   'pipes'   (animate)
> *mōhkomān*a   'knives'   (inanimate)

or add a verb: the ending of *niwēpināw*, above, signals an animate goal while that of *niwēpinēn* signals an inanimate one. In these examples, the gender is expressed by the *suffixes* and no difference is visible in the form of either noun or verb *stems*.

In the vast majority of Cree verb stems, however, the stem itself *also* expresses the gender of the noun with which the verb is used. In these two sentences,

> *ni*wāpamāw   *ospwākan.*
> see(1–3)   pipe(3)
> 'I saw a pipe(animate).'

> *ni*wāpahtēn   *mōhkomān.*
> see (1–0)   knife(0)
> 'I saw a knife(inanimate).'

we not only have the different endings -*āw* (for an animate goal) and -*ēn* (for an inanimate goal) but also clearly distinct stems:

> *wāpam-*   'see someone'   (animate goal)
> *wāpaht-*   'see something'   (inanimate goal)

*With a third person possessor one can also use the obviative distinction to test for gender. If the noun takes the obviative suffix -*a*, it is animate:

> *otōspwākan*a   'his pipe(animate)'

If it takes no suffix at all, it is inanimate:

> *omōhkomān*   'his knife(inanimate)'

In this respect, then, verbs are quite different from nouns. In nouns, gender is an inherent category and there is no need for noun stems to come in pairs. Most verbs, on the other hand, show a pattern of paired stems—to be used with nouns of either gender.

The verb forms which illustrate the expression of gender also show another important aspect of Cree verbs: that they agree not only with their actor but with their goal as well.

In English, actor nouns and verbs agree, for example, in *number*. In
> *the duck sits*,

both the noun and the verb are singular, and they are both plural in
> *the ducks sit.*

The same pattern is found in Cree:

> *apiw*   *sīsīp.*
> sit(3)   duck(3)
> 'The duck sits.'

> *apiwak*   *sīsīpak.*
> sit(3p)   duck(3p)
> 'The ducks sit.'

But in English the verb does not change at all to accommodate different goals:

> *I see one duck.*
> *I see two ducks.*

The corresponding Cree sentences signal the plural of the goal not only in the noun but in the verb as well:

> *niwāpamāw*   *pēyak*   *sīsīp.*
> see(1–3)   one   duck(3)
> 'I see one duck.'

> *niwāpamāwak*   *nīso*   *sīsīpak.*
> see(1–3p)   two   duck(3p)
> 'I see two ducks.'

Not all verb types of Cree show such full agreement with the associated nouns; but in the full two-layer forms of stems like *wāpam-* 'see someone' there is agreement as to number, gender, and obviation.

Transitive and Intransitive Stems

In Cree as in English, all verbs have an *actor* (or *subject*) but only some have a *goal* (or *object*) as well. Verbs which only have an actor are called *intransitive:*

> *apiw* : *he sits*

Verbs which occur with a goal are called *transitive:*

> *pakamahwēw* : *he hits him*

In English, intransitive and transitive verbs use the same endings:

> *he sits, he was sitting*
> *he hits him, he was hitting him*

In Cree, they use distinct sets of endings:

> *nitapi*n   'I sit'
> *nipakamahwāw*   'I hit him'

There is a further important difference in the *stems* that English and Cree use for verb forms with and without goals. In English, the same verb stem may be used transitively or intransitively:

> *John* sang.   (intransitive)
> *John* sang *three songs.*   (transitive)

Can you move?   (intransitive)
Can you move *your car?* (transitive)

Even stems which are mostly used with goals may be used intransitively:

Bill washed *the children.*
Bill washed *his hands.*
Bill washed.

I see *Mary.*
I see.

In Cree, distinct stems are used for transitive and intransitive sentences:

*ni*wăpamăw.   'I see him.'   (transitive)
*ni*wăpahtēn.   'I see it.'   (transitive)

but   *ni*wăpin.   'I see, I have vision.' (intransitive)

(or, more commonly,

　　　　　*namōýa ni*wăpin.   'I cannot see, I am blind.')

The next example,

*ni*pēhăw.   'I wait for him.' (transitive)
*ni*pēhon.   'I wait.'   (intransitive)

might also be translated as follows:

*ni*pēhăw.   'I await him.'
*ni*pēhon.   'I wait.'

The English stems *wait* (intransitive) and *await someone* (transitive) are similar but distinct much in the same way as Cree *pēbo*- 'wait' (intransitive) differs from *pēb*- 'await someone' (transitive). But while the two Cree stems are perfectly normal, the English stem *await* belongs to the formal level of style; in casual, everyday English the transitive and intransitive verbs are *wait* and *wait for someone.*

In introducing the verb forms of Cree we cannot give a full account of a verbal system well known for its rich complexity. We concentrate on those parts of the system which use the familiar inflectional elements of the outer and inner layer to signal the players and their rôles.

The Four Major Verb Types

The stems and the inflectional endings of Cree verbs fall into four major types (and many minor ones which must be left out of this discussion). The fundamental distinction is that between transitive and intransitive verbs.

Transitive verbs are used with a goal:

> *He washed the dishes.*

> *niwāpamāw iskwēw.*
> see (1–3)   woman (3)
> 'I see a woman.'

If the goal is not expressed by a full noun (such as *the dishes* or *iskwēw*), English uses a separate pronoun while Cree marks the goal by the inflectional elements of the verb:

> *He washed* **them.**

> *niwāpamā*w.
> see (1–3)
> 'I see him.'

This is most clearly seen with a plural goal:

*niwāpamā*wak *nīso* *iskwēw*ak.
see(1–3p)   two woman(3p)
'I see two women.'

*niwāpamā*wak.
see(1–3p)
'I see them.'

As this last example shows, the agreement between the verb form and the goal noun is often (but not always) expressed by inflectional endings.

 Intransitive verbs cannot be used with a goal:

Mary sleeps.

nipāw *nāpēw.*
sleep(3) man(3)
'The man sleeps.'

The actor may be expressed by a noun, as above, or by a pronoun which in Cree is included in the inflectional elements of the verb:

She sleeps.

*nipā*w.
sleep(3)
'He sleeps.'

Again, this is most clearly seen with a plural actor:

*nipā*wak *nāpēw*ak.
sleep(3p) man(3p)
'The men sleep.'

*nipā*wak.
sleep(3p)
'They sleep.'

The agreement between the verb form and the actor noun is always expressed by inflectional endings.

In the preceding example, this was illustrated for the intransitive verb *nipā-* 'sleep.' But as the following example shows, this agreement principle holds for intransitive and transitive verbs alike:

> *wāpamēw* *iskwēw* *nāpēwa.*
> see(3−(3′)) woman(3) man(3′)
> 'The woman sees a man.'

> *wāpamē***wak** *iskwēwak* *nāpēwa.*
> see(3p−(3′)) woman(3p) man(3′)
> 'The women see a man.'

There are two types of intransitive verbs depending on the gender of the *actor*. With intransitive verbs, the gender of the actor is usually expressed by both the endings **and** the shape of the stem itself:

> *ohpiki-* 'grow up' (animate)
> *ohpikin-* 'grow' (inanimate)

There are different endings and stems, therefore, for **intransitive verbs with animate actors** or **AI verbs**:

> *ohpikinwak* 'they grow up'

and for **intransitive verbs with inanimate actors** or **II verbs**:

> *ohpikinwa* 'they grow'

This last type includes a number of verbs which never take a full noun as actor:

> *kīsikāw* 'it is day'
> *wāpan* 'it is dawn'
> *pipon* 'it is winter'

In their inflection, however, these **impersonal** verbs cannot be distinguished from all other verbs of the II type.

Transitive verbs also fall into two types, but they are distinguished by the gender of the *goal*. As we have seen, the gender of the goal may be expressed either by the inflectional endings alone or, doubly, by these endings **and** the stem itself. There are different endings (and stems), therefore, for **transitive verbs with animate goals** or **TA verbs:**

> *niwāpamāw* 'I see him'

and for **transitive verbs with inanimate goals** or **TI verbs:**

> *niwāpahtēn* 'I see it'

The chart summarizes the four major verb types:

	Intransitive (gender of *actor*)	Transitive (gender of *goal*)
Animate	AI (*api-* 'sit')	TA (*wāpam* 'see s.o.')
Inanimate	II (*misā-* 'be big')	TI (*wāpaht-* 'see s.t.')

The Inflection of Intransitive Verbs

The inflectional patterns which are illustrated in this section represent the *independent mode;* the modes will be discussed in a later section.

The intransitive verbs in the independent mode use many of the inflectional elements we encountered in the inflection of nouns, but some of these elements appear in a somewhat different form. For example, the

AI verbs have *-nāwāw* instead of *-iwāw* to mark the second person plural. The inflectional elements of the AI verb are as follows:*

ni(t)-	*-n*	I
ki(t)-	*-n*	2
ni(t)-	*-nān*	Ip
ki(t)-	*-(nā)naw*	21
ki(t)-	*-nāwāw*	2p
	-w	3
	-wak	3p
	-ýiwa	3'

In the inflection of nouns, prefix-suffix combinations like *ni(t)- -(i)nān* belong to the inner layer while the plural suffix *-ak*, for example, is part of the outer layer. Inflectional elements from both layers are used to express the actor of AI verbs. Note, however, that none of the verbs illustrated in this chapter use the personal prefix of the third person, *o(t)-*.

AI Verb

Stem *api-* 'sit':

nitapin	I	'I sit'
kitapin	2	'you(sg) sit'
nitapinān	Ip	'we(excl) sit'
kitapinānaw	21	'we(incl) sit'
kitapināwāw	2p	'you(pl) sit'
apiw	3	'he sits'
apiwak	3p	'they sit'
apiýiwa	3'	'the other(s) sit(s)'

*The abbreviations of the gender-number-person-obviation categories (I, Ip, ..., 3, 3p, 3', 0, 0p, etc.) are defined in the table at the end of chapter two. In the sections which follow, 'he' or 'it' represents the *prox sg* or the *prox/obv sg*, 'they' the *prox pl* or the *prox/obv pl*, and 'the other(s)' represents the *obv*.

The great majority of AI stems end in one of the following vowels:

> *pimātisi-* 'live'
> *nikamo-* 'sing'
> *kocī-* 'try'
> *mētawē-* 'play'
> *nipā-* 'sleep'
> *pasikō-* 'get up'

But there are also a number of stems ending in the consonant *n:*

> *pimisin-* 'lie down'

The forms of *n*-stems show two discrepancies from the above example:

(a) If the ending begins with a consonant or *y*, a connective *i* is inserted:
> (*ni+pimisin+n*)
> *nipimisinin* 'I lie'

(b) If the ending is a *w* only (that is, a *w* without a vowel following), this *w* drops after a consonant:
> (*pimisin+w*)
> *pimisin* 'he lies'

The same rules apply to the *n*-stems of the II type. These rules are parallel in function to the vowel adjustment rules which are summarized at the end of chapter three.

AI Verb: n-Stems

Stem *pimisin-* 'lie (down)':

nipimisinin	I	'I lie'
kipimisinin	2	'you (sg) lie'
nipimisininān	1p	'we (excl) lie'
kipimisininaw	21	'we (incl) lie'
kipimisinināwāw	2p	'you (pl) lie'

pimisin	3	'he lies'
pimisinwak	3p	'they lie'
pimisiniýiwa	3'	'the other(s) lie(s)'

The inflection of II verbs is the only occasion where the distinction of proximate and obviative in the inanimate gender is expressed by inflectional elements:

mōhkomān	*misāw.*
knife	be-big(0)

'The knife is big(prox).'

omōhkomān	*misāýiw.*
his(3) knife	be-big(0')

'His(prox) knife is big(obv).'

The inflectional elements of the II verbs also include some which have been encountered in the inner layer of noun inflection (for example, the obviative element *-ýi-*) and some from the outer layer (for instance, the plural suffix *-a*). Since there are no first or second persons, these forms do not have personal prefixes.

The inflectional endings of the II verb are as follows:

-w	0
-wa	0p
-ýiw	0'
-ýiwa	0'p

II Verb

Stem *misā-* 'be big':

misāw	0	'it is big'
misāwa	0p	'they are big'
misāýiw	0'	'the other is big'
misāýiwa	0'p	'the others are big'

Among II stems, the proportion of stems ending in vowels is much smaller than for AI stems: approximately one-third of all II stems end in *n*. The rules which were outlined for the *n*-stems of the AI type apply without change.

II Verb: n-Stems

Stem *āýiman-* 'be difficult':

āýiman	0	'it is difficult'
āýimanwa	0p	'they are difficult'
āýimaniýiw	0'	'the other is difficult'
āýimaniýiwa	0'p	'the others are difficult'

The Inflection of Transitive Verbs

As with the intransitive verbs, the inflectional patterns which are illustrated in this section represent the *independent mode*.

The inflectional elements of the TI verb are very similar to those of the AI type:

ni(t)-	*-ēn*	I
ki(t)-	*-ēn*	2
ni(t)-	*-ēnān*	Ip
ki(t)-	*-ē(nā)naw*	2I
ki(t)-	*-ēnāwāw*	2p
	-am	3
	-amwak	3p
	-amiýiwa	3'

Like verbs of the AI type, TI verbs express only the actor by means of inflectional elements. As transitive verbs they do, of course, take a goal, and the goal may be singular or plural; for example:

pēyak	*wāskahikan*	*niwāpahtēn.*
one	house(0)	see(1–0/0p)

'I see one house.'

nīso	*wāskahikana*	*niwāpahtēn.*
two	house(0p)	see(1–0/0p)

'I see two houses.'

But the inflection of TI verbs is the same for goals of either number.

TI Verb

Stem *wāpaht-* 'see something':

niwāpahtēn	1	'I see it'
kiwāpahtēn	2	'you(sg) see it'
niwāpahtēnān	1p	'we(excl) see it'
kiwāpahtēnānaw	21	'we(incl) see it'
kiwāpahtēnāwāw	2p	'you(pl) see it'
wāpahtam	3	'he sees it'
wāpahtamwak	3p	'they see it'
wāpahtamiýiwa	3'	'the other(s) see(s) it'

The stems of TI verbs may end in *t, k, n, s,* or *h*; they never end in anything but a consonant.

TA verbs agree with two nouns, actor and goal, and therefore show the richest variety of inflectional forms. In particular, since they express two distinct persons, they also have special suffixes to show which is the actor and which the goal.

These suffixes express the grammatical category of *direction*. They signal whether the action is *direct* or *inverse*: it is **direct** if the actor ranks higher than the goal, and it is **inverse** if the goal ranks higher than the actor. The ranks, which are strictly grammatical in nature, are as follows:

person		*grammatical rank*
second	2	highest
first	1	
third		
proximate	3/3p	
obviative	3′	lowest

In our first example, the direction suffix *-ā-* indicates that the relation between the first person and the third person is *direct;* that is, the first person is the actor:

> *nipēhānānak* 'we(excl) wait for them'

The direction is *inverse* (and the first person is the goal) in the next example, where we find the suffix *-iko-* instead of *-ā-:*

> *nipēhikonānak* 'they wait for us(excl)'

Direct and inverse verb forms refer to opposite events.

The forms of the TA type fall into three sets. In the forms which will be illustrated in this section, these sets use distinct direction suffixes:

	direct	inverse
Set I	*-ā-*	*-iko-/-ikw-/-ik-*
Set II	*-ē-*	*-iko-/-ikw-/-ik-*
Set III	*-i-*	*-it-*

The three sets deal with differed person combinations. The forms of *Set I* relate a first or second person to a third person (as either actor or goal), and the third person may be singular, plural, or obviative (not illustrated) for example:

> *niwāpamāw* 'I see him'   *niwāpamāwak* 'I see them'
> *niwāpamik* 'he sees me'   *niwāpamikwak* 'they see me'

The forms of *Set II* relate one third person to another third person, for example:

wāpamēw 'he sees the other(s)'   *wāpamēwak* 'they see the other(s)'
wāpamik 'the other(s) see him'   *wāpamikwak* 'the other(s) see them'

The forms of *Set III* relate two persons, neither of which is a third person, for example:

      kiwāpamin   'you(sg) see me'
      kiwāpamitin   'I see you(sg)'

The direction suffixes are most clearly seen in the following table:

DIRECT		INVERSE	
Set I			
ni- -āwak	1–3p	*ni- -ikwak*	3p–1
ki- -āwak	2–3p	*ki- -ikwak*	3p–2
ni- -ānānak	1p–3p	*ni- -ikonānak*	3p–1p
ki- -ānawak	21–3p	*ki- -ikonawak*	3p–21
ki- -āwāwak	2p–3p	*ki- -ikowāwak*	3p–2p
Set II			
-ēw	3–(3')	*-ik*	(3')–3
-ēwak	3p–(3')	*-ikwak*	(3')–3p
-ēẏiwa	3'–(3')	*-ikoẏiwa*	(3')–3'
Set III			
ki- -in	2–1	*ki- -itin*	1–2
ki- -inān	2/2p–1p	*ki- -itinān*	1p–2/2p
ki- -ināwāw	2p–1	*ki- -itināwāw*	1–2p

The endings which begin with *i* are involved in a number of vowel adjustments after stems ending in *w*.*

If the stem-final *w* is preceded by a vowel, vowel adjustment rule 1 applies:

> *miskawēw* 'he finds the other(s)'
> (*miskaw+ik*)
> *miskāk* 'the other(s) find(s) him'

If the *w* is preceded by a consonant, vowel adjustment rule 2 applies:

> *nipakamahwāw* 'I hit him'
> (*ni+pakamahw+ik*)
> *nipakamahok* 'he hits me'

The direct endings of *Set III* do not take part in these adjustments:

> *kimiskawin* 'you(sg) find me'

But, note the inverse form:

> (*ki+miskaw+itin*)
> *kimiskātin* 'I find you(sg)'

These endings do, on the other hand, affect certain stems so that their final sound appears as *s* instead of *t*:

> (*ki+nāt+in*)
> *kināsin* 'you(sg) fetch me'

Compare the inverse form:

> *kinātitin* 'I fetch you(sg)'

While you should take note of these variations at the boundary of stem and suffix, remember that they appear only in a relatively small number of forms.

---

*A summary of the vowel adjustment rules may be found at the end of chapter three.

It would take a large number of tables to illustrate the forms of the TA verb in all their variety. The tables which follow give only the most important forms.

TA Verb: Sets I and II

Stem *wāpam-* 'see someone'

DIRECT

GOAL

	-3		$-3p$	
ACTOR				
1–	*niwāpamāw*	'I see him'	*niwāpamāwak*	'I see them'
2–	*kiwāpamāw*	'you(sg) see him'	*kiwāpamāwak*	'you(sg) see them'
1p–	*niwāpamānān*	'we(excl) see him'	*niwāpamānānak*	'we(excl) see them'
21–	*kiwāpamānaw*	'we(incl) see him'	*kiwāpamānawak*	'we(incl) see them'
2p–	*kiwāpamāwāw*	'you(pl) see him'	*kiwāpamāwāwak*	'you(pl) see them'

3–	*wāpamēw*	'he sees the other(s)'
3p–	*wāpamēwak*	'they see the other(s)'
3′–	*wāpamēyiwa*	'the other(s) see(s) another'

INVERSE

ACTOR

	$3-$		$3p-$	
GOAL				
–1	*niwāpamik*	'he sees me'	*niwāpamikwak*	'they see me'
–2	*kiwāpamik*	'he sees you(sg)'	*kiwāpamikwak*	'they see you(sg)'
–1p	*niwāpamikonān*	'he sees us(excl)'	*niwāpamikonānak*	'they see us(excl)'
–21	*kiwāpamikonaw*	'he sees us(incl)'	*kiwāpamikonawak*	'they see us(incl)'
–2p	*kiwāpamikowāw*	'he sees you(pl)'	*kiwāpamikowāwak*	'they see you(pl)'

–3	*wāpamik*	'the other(s) see(s) him'
–3p	*wāpamikwak*	'the other(s) see(s) them'
–3′	*wāpamikoyiwa*	'another sees the other(s)'

TA Verb: Set III

Stem *wāpam-* 'see someone':

DIRECT

G<small>OAL</small>			
–I		–Ip	
A<small>CTOR</small>			
2– *kiwāpamin*	'you(sg) see me'		
		kiwāpaminān 'you(sg/pl) see us(excl)'	
2p– *kiwāpaminawāw*	'you(pl) see me'		

INVERSE

A<small>CTOR</small>			
I–		Ip–	
G<small>OAL</small>			
–2 *kiwāpamitin*	'I see you(sg)'		
		kiwāpamitinān 'we(excl) see you(sg/pl)'	
–2p *kiwāpamitinawāw*	'I see you(pl)'		

The Major Modes

The verb forms which have been illustrated so far represent only one of the **modes** of Cree verbs, the **independent** mode. Since there are two further modes and a number of submodes within these modes, we can do little more than mention their existence.

The forms of the **conjunct** mode do not use personal prefixes. The endings of the AI type are intended merely to illustrate the differences between independent and conjunct endings. The corresponding forms for the other verb types may be filled in with the help of a Cree speaker or by reference to a Cree grammar (see Appendix).

AI Verb: Conjunct Mode

Stem *api-* 'sit':

apiyān	1	'as I sit'
apiyan	2	'as you(sg) sit'
apiyāhk	1p	'as we(excl) sit'
apiyahk	21	'as we(incl) sit'
apiyēk	2p	'as you(pl) sit'
apit	3	'as he sits'
apicik	3p	'as they sit'
apiẏit	3'	'as the other(s) sit(s)'

The *uses* of the independent and conjunct modes are not always easy to distinguish. The independent form appears only in constructions which can themselves stand as complete utterances:

> *nikamōw.*   'He sang.'
> *nika-nikamon.*   'I shall sing.'
> *ispatināw wāpahtam.*   'He saw the hill.'

Most sentences (but by no means all) tend to have a main verb in the independent mode.

Verbs in the conjunct mode are typically used to modify a noun:

> *wāpamēw*   *nāpēwa*   *ē-tapasīẏit.*
> see(3–(3'))   man(3')   flee(3')
> 'He saw the man fleeing.'

> *wāpamēw*   *ē-misikitiẏit*   *sīsīpa.*
> see(3–(3'))   be-big(3')   duck(3')
> 'He saw a big duck.'

But the "noun" may simply be the actor of the main verb:

ē-pimohtēt,   wāpahtam   sākahikan.
walk(3)   see(3–0)   lake(0)
'As he walked along, he saw a lake.'

Conjunct verbs may also modify the main phrase itself rather than a particular noun:

ē-wāpaniýik,   sipwēhtēw.
be-dawn(0')   leave(3)
'When it was daybreak, he left.'

In translating from Cree, independent verbs are usually rendered by English main clauses and conjunct verbs are translated by subordinate clauses. The most neutral translations for many conjunct clauses follow these patterns:

'it being such-and-such'
'as someone acted such-and-such'

For example:

'it being dawn'
'as he walked along'
ē-pipohk   'it being winter,' 'when it was winter,' 'in winter'

Sometimes a clue is provided by another word functioning like English conjunctions such as *if, while,* and *because:*

mēkwāc ē-pimohtēt,   ispatināw   wāpahtam.
while   walk(3)   hill(0)   see(3–0)
'While he walked along, he saw a hill.'

As a glance at the texts of chapter six will confirm, conjunct verb forms are extremely common in Cree.

All the conjunct forms which we have used for illustrations (here as in the sample sentences of earlier chapters) begin with the preverb ē-. This preverb, which is almost as common as the conjunct forms themselves, mainly serves to indicate one particular submode of the conjunct mode. In many contexts, the preverbs *ē-* and *kā-* are used interchangeably:

> *ē-misikitiýit*   *niska*
> be-big(3′)   goose(3′)
> 'the goose/geese which is/are big'

> *kā-misikiticik*   *sīsīpak*
> be-big(3p)   duck(3p)
> 'the ducks which are big'

Preverbs are word-like elements which come *before* the stem but *after* the personal prefixes (if any). Aside from the preverbs *ē-* and *kā-*, which are typical of the conjunct, there are many other preverbs which may occur with either mode. Among these, the time markers *kī-* and *ka-* (or its variants *kita-* and *ta-*) are the most common:

> *kita-nikamōw*   'he will sing, let him sing'
> *kī-nikamōw*   'he used to sing'

But there are also such preverbs as *wī-* 'intend to' or *ati-* 'progressively':

> *wī-nikamōw*   'he is about to sing'
> *ati-nikamōw*   'he sings along'

The Cree system of time markers is still poorly understood. All we really know is that it is quite different from the tense system of English, and we must not allow this fact to be obscured by partial resemblances.

In short, if we use such translations as 'past' for *kī-* and 'future' for *ka-*, we have to keep in mind that these translations are tentative and may well be quite inaccurate.

Conjunct clauses and time markers are only two examples from an area of Cree structure which deserves much closer study. There are many subtle distinctions within the verbal system (the conditional, for example) which have not even been mentioned.

The third major mode is the **imperative**, which is used for orders or commands. Like the verb forms of the independent order, imperative forms often occur alone as complete sentences in themselves:

> *nipā!* 'Sleep!'
> *ēkā māto!* 'Don't cry!'

Imperative forms frequently appear with the vocative form of nouns:

> *nisīmitik,* *pīhtokēk!*
> brother(voc pl) enter(2p)
> 'Little brothers, come inside!'

Among several other features, the imperative mode and the conjunct mode share the use of *ēkā* 'not.' The independent mode, on the other hand, normally uses *nama* 'not' or *namōýa* 'not.'

> *ēkā pīhtokē!* 'Don't come in!'
> *ēkā ē-wāpiyān* 'as I do not see, as I am blind'
> *nama/namōýa niwāpin* 'I do not see, I am blind'

The forms of the imperative mode all have second-person actors; in this, the first person plural inclusive is also treated as a second person since it includes the person to whom one speaks.

Al Verb: Immediate Imperative

Stem *sipwēhtē-* 'leave'

sipwēhtē	2	'leave!'
sipwēhtētān	21	'let us(incl) leave!'
sipwēhtēk	2p	'you all leave!'

TI Verb: Immediate Imperative

Stem *otin-* 'take something'

otina	2	'take it!'
otinētān	21	'let us take it!'
otinamok	2p	'you all take it!'

The imperative forms of the TA verbs also specify the goal; only some of the available forms are included in this table:

TA Verb: Immediate Imperative

Stem *asam-* 'feed someone, give someone to eat':

Set I

	GOAL	
	−3	−3p
ACTOR		
2−	*asam* 'feed him/them!'	
21−	*asamātān* 'let us feed him!'	*asamātānik* 'let us feed them!'
2p−	*asamihk* 'you all feed him!'	*asamihkok* 'you all feed them!'

Set III

	GOAL	
	−1	−1p
ACTOR		
2−	*asamin* 'feed me!'	
		asaminān 'feed us!'
2p−	*asamik* 'you all feed me!'	

The imperative forms cited above represent the **immediate** submode. Cree also has another, **delayed** imperative for commands that are to be carried out at a later time:

AI Verb: Delayed Imperative

Stem *sipwēhtē-* 'leave':

sipwēhtēhkan	2	'leave later!'
sipwēhtēhkahk	21	'let us leave later!'
sipwēhtēhkēk	2p	'you all leave later!'

The delayed imperative may be viewed as a future "tense" of the imperative:

ēkotē   *pēhihkan!*
there   await(2–1)
'Wait for me there, later!'

It is often used in conditional sentences:

asamihkan   *takosiyani.*
feed(2−1)   arrive(2)
'Give me to eat later, when you arrive.'

The tables presented in the course of this chapter are merely samples of a much larger system. In any normal speech situation you may encounter forms which have not even been mentioned in this bird's-eye view of the Cree verbal system.

For some readers, the tables and categories of this chapter will, perhaps, serve as a framework into which additional forms can be fitted as they are met. For others, even this fragmentary portrait will at least offer an impression of the rich variety and subtle complexity of verb forms in Cree.

5 Words and Sentences

A language does not consist of words alone. Words are put together to form sentences, but a sentence—whether short or long—is more than merely a sequence of words.

The existence of sentence patterns is easily demonstrated; we need only jumble the words of a perfectly ordinary English sentence. There is nothing unusual about the sentences,

> *The cat scratched Mary.*

or

> *Mary scratched the cat.*

At most, only the *event* to which the second sentence refers may be uncommon. But other sequences of the same words are totally different in kind:

> *Mary the cat scratched*
> *Scratched Mary the cat*
> *Cat Mary the scratched*
> *Mary cat scratched the*

These word-chains are simply not English sentences—even though all the words are normal, familiar English words.

At the other extreme there are structured groupings of words which are easily recognized as English sentences even though many of the individual words are not English at all. The opening stanza of Lewis Carroll's *Jabberwocky* is a well-known example:

> *'Twas brillig, and the slithy toves*
> *Did gyre and gimble in the wabe:*
> *All mimsy were the borogroves,*
> *And the mome raths outgrabe.*

We would probably not recognize a *tove*, a *rath*, or a *borogrove* if we met them on the street (or wherever else they might be found on this side of the Looking Glass) but there can be little doubt that these words are nouns: they are identified by the article *the* and, in the case of *toves*, by the verbal expression which follows, *did gyre and gimble*. The use of *were* suggests that the verb forms are plural, and this would fit well with the plural *-s* of the words which are already marked as nouns by the article *the*. The use of English words such as *'Twas, and, all* to connect the rather strange nouns, adjectives, and verbs is, of course, an essential clue, but, above all, the sentences are recognizably English because they follow the sentence patterns of English: nouns come before verbs, adjectives stand between the article and the noun, and so on. One need not know the precise identity of a *tove* or be familiar with the practice of *outgribing* to follow the interplay of inflectional structure and sentence patterns. Alice, of course, found the poem "*rather* hard to understand"; yet, as she put it: "Somehow it seems to fill my head with ideas—only I don't exactly know what they are!"

The sentence patterns of any two languages show similarities and differences of many kinds, both superficial and fundamental. Instead of a contrastive survey of English and Cree sentence patterns, however, we concentrate on the interplay of words and sentences in the two languages.

A number of the favourite sentence types of Cree have been illustrated in the examples of previous chapters, and more spontaneous and authentic examples are provided in the texts of chapter six. Many of the more complex patterns of sentence construction (the use of conjunctions, for instance) would go well beyond the scope of this book. The most important aspect of Cree sentence structure, on the other hand, has been covered in the presentation of the grammatical categories (in chapter two) and in the two long chapters on noun and verb inflection: the identification of actor and goal and the agreement between nouns and verbs.

Word Shape versus Word Order

In Cree and English alike, we have seen many examples which show that the rôles of actor and goal are identified by a combination of word order and word shape. But these two means of signalling who acts and who is at the receiving end of the action are not exploited equally: the two languages differ in the relative weight they place on word shape and word order.

The words of English have few inflectional forms (for example, *dog : dogs* or *laugh : laughs : laughing : laughed*) to indicate their syntactic rôle. Cree, by contrast, has extremely elaborate words which appear in many diverse forms when they take their place in the sentence.

Word order, on the other hand, is extremely important in an English sentence; the actor noun is identified primarily by its position before the verb. In contrast to the *fixed* word order of English, Cree word order is *free*: an actor noun, for example, is not tied to any particular position.

In both languages, then, there is a balance between word *shape* and word *order* — but the scales are tipped at opposite ends. English relies heavily on word order but makes little use of inflectional patterns. Cree, with its rich and complex patterns of changing the shape of words, does not use word order to identify the rôles within a sentence.

This see-saw relationship in the identification of sentence rôles might, in a greatly simplified form, be visualized as follows:

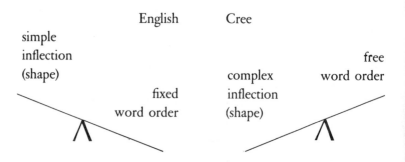

Since word order is not used to indicate the rôles within a sentence in Cree, it can be used instead for emphasis or as a stylistic device. In an English sentence, where word order is used to signal the actor, emphasis is indicated either by extra stress, as in

He *asked* **the old man.**

or by special sentence patterns:

It was the old man he asked.

In Cree, a simple change in word order will shift the emphasis:

>*kakwēcimēw*   *kisēyiniwa.*
>
>ask(3–(3'))   old-man(3')
>
>'He asked the old man.'

but

>*kisēyiniwa*   *kakwēcimēw.*
>
>old-man(3')   ask(3–(3'))
>
>'It was the old man he asked.'

The use of word order to express emphasis is also seen in questions. Questions which can be answered by *yes* or *no* are formed with the question marker *cī* (or *na*, in Swampy Cree), which follows the first full word in the sentence:

>*kakwēcimēw.*
>
>'He asked him.'

>*kakwēcimēw cī.*
>
>'Did he ask him?'

There is no special emphasis indicated in

>*kakwēcimēw cī kisēyiniwa.*
>
>'Did he ask the old man?'

but in

>*kisēyiniwa cī kakwēcimēw.*
>
>'Was it the old man he asked?' *or*
>
>'Did he ask **the old man**?'

the special emphasis placed on 'the old man' is expressed simply by a change in word order.

Verb and Noun Expressions

Neither Cree nor English words are all nouns or all verbs. English has pronouns like *he* or *that*, articles like *the* and *an*, adjectives like *big* or *enormous*, conjunctions like *when* or *although*, particles like *now* and *here*. For Cree, it has been conventional to group words according to their form rather than their function. We call *awa* a *pronoun* even where it is used much like an English article; for instance, it may indicate a specific person who has already been mentioned.

The nouns, pronouns, and verbs of Cree are inflected. All other Cree words have one and the same shape at all times; these uninflectable words are grouped together as **particles** even though their function may range from isolated time indicators, like *kīkisēpā* 'early in the morning,' to particles which connnect individual words, such as *mīna* 'and, also,' and to conjunction particles, like *kīspin* 'if' by which entire sentences are tied together.

Verbs and nouns, however, make up the skeleton of a sentence to which words of the other classes may, but need not, be added. The most important distinction, in Cree as in English, is that between nouns and verbs. Verbs occupy a central position in sentence construction, and the status of nouns in Cree sentences is evident from the elaborate system of inflectional patterns which was outlined in chapter three.

If we compare Cree sentences with their English counterparts, it is easy to see that nouns and verbs are not of equal prominence (and frequency) in the two languages. English sentences seem to contain many more nouns than their Cree counterparts. In the following sentence,

ē-wāpahk, ē-wī-māmawōpihk. : *In the morning, there will be a meeting.*

we have two English nouns, the prepositional phrase *in the (morning)* and the empty subject *there* corresponding to a Cree sentence which consists of two verb forms and nothing else. Neither of these verb forms is in the independent mode: they are two conjunct mode forms balancing each other. The Cree *ē-wāpahk* 'when day breaks' is an impersonal verb of the II type, and there is no definite actor indicated in the verb form *ē-wī-māmawōpihk* 'one intends to assemble.' No equivalents are used for English *there is* or *it is;* such relations are expressed as part of the verb forms.

Although English and Cree both use nouns and verbs, there is a clear preference for noun expressions in English and for verb expressions in Cree.

Another clear-cut discrepancy in the relation between words and sentences is the use of verb forms in Cree where English relies on adjectives. Whether English adjectives are used to modify a noun, as in

    a big dog,

or with a form of the verb *be*, as in

    it is cold,

they always correspond to Cree verbs:

    ē-misikitit   *atim*
    be-big(3)   dog(3)
    'a big dog, a dog that is big'

    kisināw
    be-cold (0)
    'it is cold weather'

The single word *kisināw* may not only carry as much information as an entire English sentence; it may also serve as a full Cree sentence all by itself.

Words as Sentences

In the course of our discussion of Cree words and sentences, we have encountered a variety of examples where an English clause or even an entire English sentence corresponds to a single word in Cree:

akohp-	'blanket'
nit*akohp*	'my blanket'
wāskahikan-	'house'
*wāskahikan*ihk	'in the house'
-īk-	'home' (dependent noun)
nī*ki*	'my home'
kī*ki*naw	'our (incl) home'
kī*ki*nāhk	'in our (incl) home'
kisinā-	'be cold weather'
ē-*kisinā*k	'when it is cold weather'
otin-	'take something'
*otin*am	'he takes something'
*otin*amētān	'let's take something!'
kakwēcim-	'ask someone'
ni*kakwēcim*ikonānak	'they ask us (excl)'
*kakwēcim*āhkēk	'you all ask him later!'

In each case, these forms and all the many others that might be formed by inflectional prefixes and suffixes are based on a single stem.

But words are not only inflected; a word may also be used as the basis for another, distinct word which usually belongs to a different word class. The English forms *cat* and *cats* are both inflected forms of the one stem *cat-*, but *catty* and *catfish* are new stems derived from that same stem; *catty* is an example of **derivation** while *catfish* combines two stems into a **compound**.

Since the derivational and compounding patterns of Cree are every bit as complex and varied as the inflectional patterns of Cree nouns and verbs, a few examples will have to suffice:

> *wāpam-*   'see someone'
> *wāpamiso-* 'see oneself'

> *wāpam-*   'see someone'
> *kitāpam-*   'look at someone'

These two examples show the derivation of one stem from another full stem. In the following instances, we begin with a **root** (which cannot occur by itself) and add several diverse derivational suffixes:

> *mākw-*   'press together' (root)

> *mākwam-*   'press someone in one's mouth, chew someone'
> *mākwaht-* 'press something in one's mouth, chew something'

> *mākwahw-* 'press someone with a tool'
> *mākwah-*   'press something with a tool'

And, finally, if someone were held down by a (fallen) tree, one might say
> *mākwāskohw-* 'press someone, in tool fashion, as a tree'
In the compound
> *paskwāwi-mostos* 'buffalo'
the first part is based on the noun stem
> *paskwāw-* 'prairie'
which in turn includes the root
> *paskw-* 'bald, bare'
In some instances, the derived stems are used as the basis of further derivations:

> *nōtin-*   'fight someone'
> *nōtinikē-*   'fight with people'
> *nōtinikēstamaw-*   'fight with people on someone's behalf'
> *nōtinikēstamāso-*   'fight with people on one's own behalf'

Quite commonly, verbs are derived from nouns which are themselves derived from verbs:

nīmih-   'make someone dance'
nīmihito-   'dance' (verb)
nīmihitōwin-   'a dance' (noun)
nīmihitōwinihkē-   'arrange a dance, give a dance'

None of these forms have been made up as illustrations; all four layers of the last example occur in text A of chapter six.

6   Literature

Sounds are merely building blocks for words, words are combined into sentences, and even sentences are not the largest units of speech. Although one-word sentences and single-sentence statements are common, the sentences we utter are usually part of longer, connected speech events. These are easiest to recognize when they are formal and begin with

Mr. Chairman, Ladies, and Gentlemen, ...

or

C'mon now, you guys, listen to me ...

and the like. But casual exchanges have just as much structure:

You know what, Mom? When I got to school today, this kid, you know, he threw a snowball at me.

In the preceding dinner-time report, the first sentence cannot stand alone; it is a means for attracting attention and focussing it on the narrative which follows. In a similar fashion, every exchange of question and answer is a structured speech event:

What time is it?
I make it twenty past.

Neither of these sentences normally occurs without the other.

In any language, speech events or **connected discourses** offer a more complete picture of language use than isolated phrases or sentences. The more complete the picture, however, the more complex as well. The above snowball story began in the past tense, but in English even a past event is often reported in the present tense:

> *... this kid, you know, he threw a snowball at me.*
> *So I threw one back at him. And then he* **grabs** *a piece of ice,*
> **breaks** *it off, and tried to hit me with it.*

In a similar fashion, we will see changes from plural to singular and back again in Cree texts. Some grammatical features, in particular the obviative, are much more fully used in connected discourse.

Normal, spontaneous speech is an excellent source of information about language. Whether formal or casual, texts also tell us a great deal about the people who are speaking and the times that are being discussed. The two Cree texts which follow contain much cultural and historical information. At the same time they are authentic examples of Cree literary expression.

Literature without Writing

The term *literature* may seem odd for a society which does not spend much time and effort on writing; for most people, the word *literature* evokes novels, Shakespeare, and libraries. Yet much of world literature started out as *oral literature;* the Psalms, the epics of Homer, and many other literary works that we are now accustomed to read were originally recited or chanted orally. As pointed out earlier, writing is a fairly recent invention, and in many societies the storage and transmission of information relies on human memory rather than on notebooks.

Stories have been handed down for centuries in every society in the world, and the texts of the Cree are no exception. Members of pre-literate societies worked harder at training their memories, and many of the texts that have been kept alive in this way are extremely long. Some types of texts may be shortened, embellished, or changed in other ways to fit the style of a particular narrator or the interests of a particular audience, but where faithful reproduction is important texts can be recited with great accuracy.

Orally transmitted texts differ in a variety of ways from stories which were written down from the outset. A single example will have to suffice. When reporting speech, most modern writing systems use quotation marks. In oral literature the beginning and end of reported speech is typically marked by words meaning "I said," "he thought," etc. In sentences (17) and (21) of text B below, the quoted passage is closed off by the verb *ē-itēyihtahk* '[this is] what he thought'; in sentence (2) of text A, the form *itēyihtam* 'so he thought' begins the reported speech and ends it as well. In the course of a dialogue, as in text A, verb forms like *itwēw* 'so he/she said' are repeated over and over. Spoken English uses similar devices: in formal speech a quotation is often ended with the word *unquote* (and a change in tone) and in casual story-telling we encounter the phrase *I says*, which may be non-standard but is certainly not uncommon.

Cree Literature

The Cree recognize two major genres or types of literature. Text A is an example of the *ātayōhkēwin;* text B is an *ācimōwin*.

Like most technical terms, these words are difficult to translate. For *ātayōhkēwin,* 'sacred story' suggests the legendary, supernatural, and mythological aspects of many texts. In their world, for example, animals and many other parts of nature have personalities and share man's ability to speak. That these stories may only be told under well-defined circumstances (never in summer!) also indicates their separate status.

As text A shows, however, the 'sacred stories' do not portray the lives of saints. They deal with perfectly ordinary situations and often in a very human way. In many cases, entertainment is combined with education: while Wisahkechahk succeeds in getting himself a hefty meal in text A, there is a second part to the story where his deceitfulness receives its just deserts. Many Wisahkechahk stories provide mythological origins for features of the natural environment. In our story, for instance, the hell-diver duck opens its eyes (which are red) and has its rump kicked so that it becomes crooked.

Wisahkechahk is trickster and dupe at once; he tries to trick anyone he meets in his wanderings and usually ends up the loser himself. Not surprisingly, 'sacred stories' in which he plays the major rôle are particularly popular.

All texts which are not classed as *ātayōhkēwin* are considered *ācimōwin*. These 'tales' or 'stories' deal with the present world. They may range from a report of yesterday's hunting trip to an account of some inexplicable event which might well involve the supernatural; but here the supernatural is a feature of the factual world. The age which preceded the colonial period is a favourite subject of *ācimōwina*.

Literary Form

In either genre, literary style is more formal than the language of daily conversation. Elaborate, carefully constructed sentences and concern for the right word are typical of formal style—and not in Cree alone. When, in text B, the Blackfoot seek shelter in the woods, the narrator uses neither "go" nor "run" but a word with a very specific meaning appropriate to the situation: *sēskisiwak* 'they moved into the woods' (B22). The *sēskāmōwak* of B14, while built on the same root *sēsk-*, includes an additional element *-āmo-* to indicate flight: 'they fled into the woods.'

The formality of narrative style is also expressed by a feature which has no direct parallel in English. In many instances, the text begins or ends with an explicit mention of the genre terms, *ātayōhkēwin* or *ācimōwin* (as in the case of A49 and B35).

The plot of an *ātayōhkēwin* or sacred story is essentially a matter of tradition, and many of the narrative details are also highly conventionalized. Although the framework is given, however, the rôle of the narrator is still fundamentally distinct from that of an actor who recites a predetermined text. Voices, pauses, flourishes, and special effects are equally important in characterizing, for example, the villainy of Richard III and Wisahkechahk's greed (text A) as he prepares his murderous scheme. But the actor who plays Richard has Shakespeare's written text. The narrator who re-creates Wisahkechahk single-handedly manages the different strands of the action, decides when the figures are moved from background to centre stage and off again, and, above all, re-creates the wording itself.

The dramatic structure of an *ācimōwin* or tale depends to an even greater degree on the choice of the individual narrator rather than on collective knowledge. In relating an encounter between Cree and Blackfoot warriors, the historical narrative B effectively displays the extraordinary bravery of *owīhkasko-kisēyin* 'Sweet-Grass.' The authenticity of the report is clearly an important issue, since it is explicitly confirmed in B36. But the tale itself is framed (B1, B34) by opening and closing passages whose symmetry offers a classical example of the narrator's art:

> *kayās mitoni kisēyiniw ēwako okimāw.*
> 'In the time of the men of long ago he was chief.'

> *ēwako ē-kī-okimāwit, kayās kisēyiniwak.*
> 'He was chief among the men of old.'

The Texts

The stories which follow were told in 1925 by *kā-kīsikāw-pīhtokēw* 'Coming-Day' at Sweet Grass, Saskatchewan, and written down by Leonard Bloomfield.* They are taken (with permission) from the text collections, edited

*For a sketch of Coming-Day and his narrative performance, see Bloomfield's introduction to *Sacred Stories of the Sweet Grass Cree.*

by Bloomfield, which are discussed in the Appendix, but the spelling has been normalized and adjusted to fit the orthography of this book.

A detailed linguistic analysis of these texts would fill a book of its own.

While a word-by-word translation might be useful for an intensive study of these texts, literal translations are rarely suitable for reading. With its formal and slightly archaic style, Bloomfield's translation (which has been changed only in minor ways) reflects the literary character of the Cree texts.

(A)

kā-kīsikāw-pīhtokēw:

1 kītahtawē ē-pimohtēt wīsahkēcāhk—nōhtēhkatēw māka mīna—ē-pimohtēt, kā-wāpamāt sīsīpa, ēkwa niska mihcēt, sīsīpa.

2 ēkosi ōmisi itēyihtam: "tānisi k-ēsi-nipahakik?" itēyihtam.

3 kītahtawē kā-wāpahtahk sākahikanis, ēkota sisonē nipīhk kā-wāpahtahk asisiya. 4 otinam, ē-titipinahk. 5 mistahi tahkopitam, ē-nayahtahk, ē-sipwēhtēt. 6 sīsīpa ita k-āyāyit, ēkota cīki ē-pimohtēt, kā-wāpamikot sīsīpa.

7 ōmisi itwēwak sīsīpak: "hā, kistēsinaw!" itwēwak; "kīkway kā-nayahtahk?" ēkosi itwēwak.

8 "mahti nika-kakwēcimāw," itwēw awa sīsīp.

9 "ēhaʔ," itwēwak.

(A) The Shut-Eye Dancers

Coming-Day:

¹ Once upon a time, as Wisahkechahk was tramping along—as usual he was hungry—as he was tramping along, he saw some ducks and many geese, and ducks.

² Then this was what he thought: "How shall I kill them?" he thought.

³ Presently he saw a little lake, and by the water's edge some weeds. ⁴ He took them and rolled them up. ⁵ He tied up a great bundle of them, took it on his back, and went off. ⁶ When he came walking close to where the ducks were, they caught sight of him.

⁷ The ducks said, "Ho, our big brother! What is that he's carrying on his back?" they said.

⁸ "Suppose I ask him," said one duck.

⁹ "Very well," they said.

¹⁰ "nistēsē, kīkway kā-nayahtaman?"

¹¹ āhci piko pimohtēw. ¹² tāpiskōc ēkā ē-pēhtawāt, āhci piko pimohtēw.

¹³ āsay mīna sīsīp ōmisi itēw: "nistēsē, kīkway kā-nayahtaman?"

¹⁴ ēkoyikohk nīpawiw wīsahkēcāhk.

¹⁵ "mā," itwēw, "kīkway kā-nayahtaman?"
¹⁶ "wā, pasakwāpisimōwina!" itwēw wīsahkēcāhk.

¹⁷ "kīkway pasakwāpisimōwin?" itwēw sīsīp.

¹⁸ wīsahkēcāhk ōmisi itwēw: "nīmināna," itēw.

¹⁹ "nīmihinān," itwēw sīsīp; "nika-pasakwāpisimonān!"

²⁰ "hay, hay!" itwēw wīsahkēcāhk; "ā, miywāsin ē-kitimākinawiyēk, nisīmitik! nama awiyak nitāpwēhtāko, tē-nīmihitocik, kayās ē-kī-asotamān ta-nīmihitōwinihkēyān," itwēw wīsahkēcāhk; "ēkosi pē-kapāk."

²¹ ta-sipwēhtēwak ēkwa sīsīpak mīna niskak.
²² kahkiyaw itohtēwak.

²³ ōmisi itwēw wīsahkēcāhk: "maci-kakēpātisak, ninōhtēhkatēwā! mistahi nika-mīcison!" itēyihtam wīsahkēcāhk.

²⁴ ē-apit, ēkota takohtēyiwa.

¹⁰ "Big brother, what is that you're carrying on your back?"

¹¹ He kept right on walking. ¹² Just as if he had not heard, he kept on walking.

¹³ Again the duck asked him, "Big brother, what is it you're carrying on your back?"

¹⁴ Only then did Wisahkechahk stand still.

¹⁵ "Say," it said, "what is it you're carrying?"

¹⁶ "Why, Shut-Eye Dances!" said Wisahkechahk.

¹⁷ "What is a Shut-Eye Dance?" said the duck.

¹⁸ Wisahkechahk spoke thus: "A saltatory rite," he told it.

¹⁹ "Do you give us a dance," said the duck; "We shall dance the Shut-Eye Dance!"

²⁰ "Splendid!" cried Wisahkechahk; "Oh, it is fine that you have taken pity on me, little brothers! No one has given heed to me until now, and danced, when long ago I had pledged myself to give a ritual dance," said Wisahkechahk; "So then, come ashore."

²¹ Off went the ducks and geese. ²² All of them came.

²³ Thus spoke Wisahkechahk: "Hopeless ninnies, I've been starving! I shall have a big meal!" thought Wisahkechahk.

²⁴ They came to where he sat.

²⁵ "ā, āstamitik, nisīmitik!" itwēw wīsahkēcāhk.

²⁶ ēkwa ē-sipwēhtēt, ē-sakāyik ē-itohtēt, mihta ita
ē-mihcēniyiki, ēkota takohtēw.

²⁷ "hā, nisīmitik, otinamok mihta," itwēw.

²⁸ tāpwē otinamwak mihcēt, ēkwa ē-osīhtācik wīkiwāw,
ēkota ē-apahkwēcik ōhō asisiya. ²⁹ apisāsiniyiw
iskwāhtēmis.

³⁰ "hā, ēkwa, nisīmitik, pīhtokēk," itwēw; "nīkān
ta-pīhtokēwak niskak ēkwa kā-misikiticik sīsīpak," itwēw;
"cikēmā ēwakonik ē-okimāwicik," itwēw.

³¹ wēskwāhtēmihk ēkosi ōmisi itapiyiwa, ēwakonik
niskak. ³² nētē iskwāhtēmihk, ēwakonik ē-apisīsisicik ēkota
apiwak. ³³ ēkwa kipaham ōma iskwāhtēm awa
wīsahkēcāhk, "ēkā ka-wayawīcik," ē-itēyihtahk. ³⁴ ēkwa
mātōw wīsahkēcāhk.

³⁵ "nisīmitik, kinanāskomitināwāw, ē-kīsihtāyēk ōma
mīkiwāhp; ēkā awiyak ē-kitimākinawit, kīyawāw
kā-kitimākinawiyēk," itwēw, ē-mātot.

³⁶ ēkosi pōni-mātōw.

³⁷ ōmisi itwēw wīsahkēcāhk: "hā, nisīmitik, ōta
tāwayihk nika-nīpawin; nika-nikamon; nikamoyāni,
ka-nīmihitonāwāw; iyikohk pōni-nikamoyāni, ēkoyikohk
ka-tōhkāpināwāw; kīspin manitōw nipēcimāw, 'hwē hwē
hwē!' nik-ētwān; ēkota sōhki ka-nīmihitonāwāw,
pēhtawiyēko, ēkosi itwēyāni."

³⁸ "ēha?," itwēwak.

²⁵ "Ha, come here, little brothers!" said Wisahkechahk.

²⁶ Setting out and making for a clump of trees, he came
to where there were plenty of sticks for a fire.

²⁷ "Ha, little brothers, take up some faggots," he said.

²⁸ Accordingly they took up a plenty and built
themselves a lodge which they thatched with those weeds.
²⁹ The little doorway was very small.

³⁰ "Ha, now, little brothers, come inside," he said; "First
the geese and the big ducks will come in," he said;
"Especially those who are chiefs," he said.

³¹ Accordingly these, the geese, sat like this, at the far
end, facing the door. ³² Over at the other end, by the
door sat the little fellows. ³³ Then that Wisahkechahk
blocked up the doorway, thinking "So that they can't get
out." ³⁴ Then Wisahkechahk wept.

³⁵ "Little brothers, I thank you for having built this
lodge; when no one took pity on me, it was you who
pitied me," he spoke, weeping.

³⁶ Then he ceased weeping.

³⁷ Thus spoke Wisahkechahk: "Now, little brothers,
here in the centre I shall stand; I shall sing; when I sing,
you will dance; [you will close your eyes]; not until I cease
singing will you open your eyes; when I summon the
spirit-power, I shall say 'Hwē, hwē, hwē!'; then you will
dance with all your might, when you hear me call thus."

³⁸ "Very well," they answered.

³⁹ ēkwa mistik tahkonam wīsahkēcāhk, nīpiya
ē-kayāsayiwiyiki ē-takopitēyiki, ōmisi ē-isiwēpinahk,
ē-sēwēpayiyiki, tāpiskōc sasawihyākan, ōhi nīpiya. ⁴⁰ ēkosi
ēkwa nikamōw.

⁴¹ ōmisi itwēw:

"pasakwāpisimōwina
nipēciwitān!"

ēkosi itwēw, ē-nikamot.

⁴² ēkwa ōhi kahkiyaw ē-pasakwāpicik, ē-nīmihitocik,
kītahtawē, "hwē hwē!" itwēw wīsahkēcāhk, ē-otināt
ē-misikitiyit niska, ē-kīskikwēpitāt. ⁴³ ēkosi
ē-ati-wāsakāmēt, tahki ē-nikamot, ē-ati-kīskikwēpitāt niska
ōhi mīna
sīsīpa kā-misikitiyit. ⁴⁴ nētē iskwāhtēmihk ē-nīmihitot
sihkihp, ēwako ē-pēhtahk kīkway, ē-napatē-tōhkāpit,
ē-nīmihitot, kā-wāpamāt wīsahkēcāhkwa ē-ati-nipahāyit.

⁴⁵ "īyahā!" itwēw, "māka mīna kimēscihikonaw
wīsahkēcāhk!" itwēw.

⁴⁶ ē-tōhkāpicik kotakak, ōmisi itwēw wīsahkēcāhk:
"kīkway ōma ita kē-pētāyān nīmihitōwin, kakēpātisicik?
ninōhtēhkatā!" itēw ōhi sīsīpa.

⁴⁷ wayawīyāmōwak kotakak, ē-tapasīcik.

* * *

⁴⁸ ē-ta-tahkiskawāt sihkihpa, "hā, ōtē nīkān ayīsiyiniw

³⁹ Then Wisahkechahk took hold of a branch that had old leaves on it which rustled when he swung it, like this [gesture], just like a bell, those leaves. ⁴⁰ Thereupon he began singing.

⁴¹ These were his words:

> "Shut-Eye Dances
> I bring here!"

were the words of his song.

⁴² Then, when they all had closed their eyes and were dancing, presently, "Hwē, hwē!" went Wisahkechahk, taking hold of a big goose and wringing its neck. ⁴³ In this way he kept on circling round, singing all the while, and, as he went, wringing the necks of the geese and of the big ducks. ⁴⁴ Over yonder by the door danced Hell-Diver, and when he heard something or other, and opened one eye as he danced, there he saw Wisahkechahk killing one after another.

⁴⁵ "Yah!" he cried, "It's the same old story, Wisahkechahk is killing us off!"

⁴⁶ When the others opened their eyes, Wisahkechahk said: "What sort of dance would I be bringing, you blockheads? I was hungry, that's all!" he said to these ducks.

⁴⁷ They fled out of doors, the others, trying to get away.

* * *

⁴⁸ When he kicked Hell-Diver, "Now then, ahead in

kit-ōhpikiw; ka-wāpamik ōma kā-nanapotōkanēskātān;
'sihkihp' kik-ēsiyīhkātikwak; namoya ka-miyosin; osām
kikisiwāhin ē-wīhtaman, ē-tōhkāpiyan," itēw.

* * *

⁴⁹ ēkosi ēkoyikohk ēwako ātayōhkēwin.

(B)

kā-kīsikāw-pīhtokēw:

¹ kayās mitoni kisēyiniw ēwako okimāw. ² ōma
nakīwacīhk ōta wīkiwak. ³ kītahtawē kīkisēpā otinēw
misatimwa; wiyahpitēw, ē-tēhtapit; sipwēhtēw,
ē-papāmohtēt. ⁴ mēkwā ē-pimohtēt, ispatināw wāpahtam,
ē-āmaciwēyit ayīsiyiniwa, nāpēwa. ⁵ ēkwa kitāpamēw,
kitāpākan ē-kanawāpākanēhikēyit, ayīsiyiniwa
ē-nanātawāpamāyit. ⁶ kiskēyimēw ayahciyiniwa. ⁷ ēkwa
opāskisikan pīhtāsōw; mōskīstawēw ē-pimisiniyit. ⁸ ēkwa
ē-kī-kiskēyihtahk awa ayahciyiniw, nēhiyawa
ē-mōskīstākot, tapasīw; ē-sakāyik kotēskamōw. ⁹ ēkosi
pāskiswēw nēhiyaw. ¹⁰ namoya matwēwiw pāskisikan.
¹¹ ēkota ē-sēskāmot, ēkota ohci mātāwisiwak nīsosāp
ayahciyiniwak. ¹² ēkwa nēhiyaw ē-pēyakot mōskīstawew,
ē-wī-nōtināt, ē-wī-pāskiswāt. ¹³ tapasīwak ōki
ayahciyiniwak, ē-pēyakoyit ē-kostācik, ē-pā-pāskisokocik.
¹⁴ kotak sakāw ēkota mīna sēskāmōwak. ¹⁵ āsay mīna
mātāwisiwak, ē-pimipahtācik. ¹⁶ ēkwa awa nēhiyaw
ē-tēhtapit, ēkotē mīkiwāhpa, mitoni ē-mihcēticik
nēhiyawak, ēkotē ē-itisahwāt. ¹⁷ ayahciyiniw "ēkotē
nika-pimātisin" ē-itēyihtahk, namoya kiskēyihtam
ayīsiyiniwa nēhiyawa ē-mihcētiyit ēkota k-ētohtēcik.
¹⁸ iyikohk
ē-wāpamācik nēhiyawa, ēkoyikohk wāyonīwak,
ē-kī-wāpamācik mihcēt nēhiyawa.

future time mortal man will grow up; he will see here on you where I have kicked your rump crooked; 'Hell-Diver' they will call you; you will not be handsome; too much have you angered me by telling this and by opening your eyes," he told him.

* * *

⁴⁹ And so this is the end of this sacred story.

(B) How Sweet-Grass Became Chief

Coming-Day:

¹ In the time of the men of long ago he was chief. ² Here at Sweet Grass they dwelt. ³ One morning, he took a horse; he saddled it and mounted; he set out to roam. ⁴ As he went along he saw someone climbing a hill, a man. ⁵ He observed him, watching through a spyglass, this man who was looking for people. ⁶ He knew him for a Blackfoot. ⁷ He loaded his gun and attacked him as he [the Blackfoot] lay on the ground. ⁸ When the Blackfoot perceived that a Cree was attacking him, he fled; he hid in the bushes. ⁹ The Cree tried to shoot him. ¹⁰ But the gun did not go off. ¹¹ From the place where he had fled into the woods, twelve Blackfoot came out upon the trail. ¹² The lone Cree attacked them, wanting to do battle and shoot them. ¹³ The Blackfoot fled, fearing the one Cree who was shooting at them. ¹⁴ They fled into another wood. ¹⁵ Again they came forth in their course. ¹⁶ But the Cree on his horse was driving them to where the Cree were many in their tents. ¹⁷ The Blackfoot meanwhile, thinking, "In this direction I shall escape," did not know that there were many people, many Cree in the place to which they were going. ¹⁸ When they saw the Cree, they turned, at the sight of the many Cree.

[19] ēkwa pēyak awa nīsosāp ayahciyiniwa ē-nawaswātāt,
ē-sakāyik ēwako mōskīstamwak sīpīsis. [20] ēkota
pahkopēwak, ē-āsōwahahkik. [21] ēkota nipīhk kōkīw pēyak
ayahciyiniw, ē-kāsōt, "namoya nika-wāpamik nēhiyaw"
ē-itēyihtahk. [22] kotakak ōki tapasīwak pēyakosāp; kotak
sakāw ēkotē sēskisiwak. [23] ēkotē ēkwa nēhiyawak
wīhkwēskawēwak, tāpiskōc wātihkān ē-osīhtācik
ayahciyiniwak, ē-nōtinikēcik. [24] ekwa ōki nēhiyawak
kisiwāk ē-itohtēcik ita ē-ayāyit ayahciyiniwa, ēkwa ēwako
kā-papā-nawaswātāt, ēwako nīkānohtēw, tāpiskōc aya
simākanis-okimāw, ēkwa ōki ayahciyiniwak kisiwāk
ē-wāpamācik nēhiyawa ēkwa ōma wātihkān ōma k-āyācik.
[25] ēkwa nēhiyawak ēkota nīpawiwak wātihkānihk cīki.
[26] ēkwa pēyak nēhiyaw—tāpiskōc ōma mistik ōta—
ē-tā-tahkamāt mōhkomān ohci ayahciyiniwa; ēwako pēyak
nēhiyaw kā-tōtahk. [27] ēkosi ēkwa kahkiyaw nēhiyawak
pīhtokēwak wātihkānihk, mōhkomān ē-tahkonahkik,
nēhiyawak ōhi ayahciyiniwa ē-tā-tahkamācik mōhkomān
ohci. [28] nipahēwak; kahkiyaw nama awiyak pimātisiw
pēyakosāp aniki ayahciyiniwak. [29] ēkosi ēkwa mōhkomān
ohci ē-manisamawācik, ostikwāniyiwa ē-manisamwācik
nēhiyawak. [30] ēkosi poyōwak. [31] ayis mēscihēwak; ēwako
ohci kā-poyocik. [32] ēkota ohci ana kā-pēyakot, nistam
kā-wāpamāt ōhi ayahciyiniwa, ēwako ohci mistahi
kī-okimāwiw. [33] ēwako ōma swīt-kwās isiyīhkāsōw,
owīhkasko-kisēyin isiyīhkāsōw. [34] ēwako ē-kī-okimāwit,
kayās kisēyiniwak.

[35] ēwako kayās ācimōwin. [36] ēwako otaskīhk
kā-pēhtamān ōma otācimōwin, ēkota ē-apiyān otaskīhk
ōma kā-otinamān ācimōwin. [37] ēkosi.

¹⁹ Then, as the one was pursuing the twelve Blackfoot, in a wooded place they made for a creek. ²⁰ They went into the water to cross. ²¹ There one of the Blackfoot ducked under the water to hide, thinking, "The Cree will not see me." ²² The other eleven fled; they went into another wood. ²³ There the Cree surrounded them, the Blackfoot making a kind of trench as they fought.
²⁴ When the Cree went near to where the Blackfoot were, then he who had pursued them, he went in the lead, like an officer, and the Blackfoot saw the Cree come near the trench where they were. ²⁵ And the Cree stood there close to the pit. ²⁶ Then one Cree—holding it like this stick [here the narrator gestures]—with his knife began to stab the Blackfoot; one Cree did this. ²⁷ Thereupon all the Cree began to enter the trench, knife in hand, stabbing one Blackfoot after another. ²⁸ They slew them; not one of those eleven Blackfoot was left alive. ²⁹ Then with their knives they scalped them; the Cree cut the scalps from their heads. ³⁰ Then they ceased. ³¹ They had finished them all; that was why they ceased. ³² For this exploit he who had gone alone, and had first seen those Blackfoot, he became a great chief for this exploit. ³³ He was called "Sweet-Grass," his name was *owīhkasko-kisēyin*. ³⁴ He was chief among the men of old.

³⁵ This is a story of long ago. ³⁶ In his land I heard this story of him; even here where I sit, in this his land I learned this story. ³⁷ That is all.

Conclusion

A sketch of any language is bound to include some parts which are difficult to follow and may have to be read more than once. Yet, if we are realistic about the nature of language we have to recognize that in our study of Cree structure we have at best scratched the surface. Language is an extremely complex system, and the Cree language is no exception. On the other hand, we can take hope from the fact that man is endowed with a remarkable capacity for learning a language; while this ability is most spectacular in children, it is by no means restricted to them.

In this book we have presented the more important features of the Cree language, and the interested reader can build on this foundation in a variety of ways. Being more conscious of his own language and of the differences that exist across languages, perhaps he will want to explore the intricacies of Cree more deeply. At least, he (which is once more used to refer to persons of either sex) should have a better understanding of the problems which we all—speakers of Cree or English—face when we try to cope with a new language. And, finally, with this background he is ready to begin the challenging and rewarding task of actually *learning to speak Cree*.

Appendix:
Supplementary Readings

In a small book, the structure of a language can only be sketched in rough outline. Readers interested in a more detailed analysis of Cree might turn to linguistic studies of particular topics or to a reference grammar.

For those who want to learn Cree, sets of lessons have been developed to guide the teacher as well as the student. There are also several other publications dealing with practical matters, especially sounds and writing.

A fairly comprehensive review of writings on Cree may be found in

Wolfart, H. Christoph. "The Current State of Cree Language Studies." *Western Canadian Journal of Anthropology* 3, no. 4 (1973): 37–55.

Unfortunately, there is no adequate dictionary of Cree at this time.

Practical Works

A set of lessons always reflects the circumstances under which it was prepared: the specific purpose, the students, the dialect, the teacher. But the three textbooks listed below (and there may well be others) have an important feature in common: since they have been designed on the basis of intensive linguistic analysis, they include information *about* Cree in the lessons for learning *how to speak and understand* Cree.

Ideally, any language should be taught by native speakers who have been specially trained in language teaching. However, since such teachers are rarely available for Cree,* Ellis's lessons are accompanied by a set of tapes. In its function as a practical language course, his book is designed for use with a teacher who is fluent in Cree or with the tapes: "any attempt to proceed without either one or the other will render the material useless or even misleading."

Where the Ellis course can be supplemented by conversation and additional practice with Cree speakers (especially in the specific target dialect selected), a serious student should be able to acquire a fair control of Cree by this method; but it deserves to be stressed that, even more than in a classroom situation, progress in a programmed course depends crucially on the student's own ability and energy.

This brings us to a very important question: What about dialects? We have already mentioned the great variety of Cree dialects, and any one textbook can obviously present only one. If several dialects were introduced at once, the confusion would become intolerable.

But the character of a language does not depend on the absolute identity of all words and sounds across all dialects; rather, the crucial characteristic is its underlying grammatical structure, and dialect differences may be compared to the very small part of an iceberg that shows above the water. In spite of obvious differences, the basic structure of English, for example, is the same in Winnipeg, London, or New Orleans. Once the basic structure of a language has been learned, the minor and superficial adjustments required for a particular area dialect are easy to add.

Edwards, Mary. *Cree, an Intensive Language Course.* Meadow Lake, Saskatchewan: Northern Canada Evangelical Mission, 1954.
Basically sound; similar to Ellis's *Spoken Cree* but much less comprehensive and without tapes. Edwards uses the Plains dialect.

---

*The Faculty of Education at Brandon University, Brandon, Manitoba, is one of the few places where Cree speakers are being trained as language teachers.

Ellis, C. Douglas. *Spoken Cree, West Coast of James Bay.* Toronto: Anglican Book Centre, 1962.

This is a pedagogically designed, highly structured instruction program. The tapes comprise approximately twenty-five hours' worth of carefully chosen materials, and while such a book-and-tape course is clearly not the ultimate in language instruction it is a most important resource to have for any language.

Ellis's course is based on the Swampy dialect of Fort Albany, Ontario, which is also represented by the voices heard on the tapes. While Swampy Cree is an *n*-dialect, the spelling (but only the spelling) in the textbook reflects Anglican usage which is based on the Moose Factory dialect. Thus, wherever the textbook has *l* the tapes have *n*, and this is the usage the student should follow.

Voorhis, Paul H., William Ballantyne, et al. *A Cree Phrase Book.* Brandon, Manitoba: Brandon University Bookstore, 1972.

Although still only in a preliminary edition, this set of lessons was developed by and for a group of Cree-speaking language teachers. It represents the Swampy Cree of northern Manitoba and marks as *ń* those sounds of Swampy Cree which correspond to *y* (that is, *ý*) in Plains Cree; for example, *nińa* 'I.'

The sounds of Cree (and English) and the writing of Cree sounds are practical problems which stand at the beginning of any language learning effort. While Soveran's manual is primarily intended for Cree-speaking students of English, it may also be used as a contrastive study of Cree and English sounds:

Soveran, Marilylle. *From Cree to English. Part I: The Sound System.* Saskatoon: Indian and Northern Curriculum Resources Centre, University of Saskatchewan, 1966.

Further examples of sounds in various combinations and how they might be written are given in

Pentland, David H. *Nēhiyawasinahikēwin: A Standard Orthography for the Cree Language.* Regina: Saskatchewan Indian Federated College, 1977.

The argument for a standardized orthography using Roman letters is most clearly and most forcefully presented by Ellis:

Ellis, C. Douglas. "A Proposed Standard Roman Orthography for Cree." *Western Canadian Journal of Anthropology* 3, no. 4 (1973): 1–37.
It is based on a detailed evaluation of all the writing systems which have been used for Cree.*

Linguistics and Language Learning

Learning a second language is both a learning problem and a linguistic problem. The following books discuss both aspects of the problem and provide further references:

Moulton, William G. *A Linguistic Guide to Language Learning.* New York: Modern Language Association of America, 1966.

Larson, Donald N., and William A. Smalley. *Becoming Bilingual: A Guide to Language Learning.* New Canaan, Connecticut: Practical Anthropology, 1972.

Rivers, Wilga, and M.S. Temperley, *A Practical Guide to the Teaching of English as a Second or Foreign Language.* Oxford: Oxford University Press, 1978.

Practical aspects of language learning are also taken up in

Anishinaabe Giigidowin: A Bilingual Newsletter for Ojibwe and Potawatomi Language Teachers. Thunder Bay, Ontario: Native Teacher Education Program, Lakehead University.

---

*The *keywords* presented in chapter one (page 4) were first tried out at a conference (organized by S. Nancy LeClaire, **a.s.v.**) held in Edmonton in 1975.

Although written primarily for (and by) speakers of Ojibwa, it is an excellent source of information for anyone dealing with Cree. Since the two languages are closely related, they share many pedagogical problems.

For Cree, unfortunately, there is nothing to match the consistency and reliability of

Nichols, John, and Earl Nyholm, eds. *Ojibwewi-Ikidowinan: An Ojibwe Word Resource Book.* St. Paul, Minnesota: Minnesota Archaeological Society, 1979.
Aside from a dictionary of thirty-five hundred words and stems, this book includes essays on the Ojibwa language in general, on Ojibwa sounds and writing, and a list of other works on Ojibwa.

If Cree is to be approached as the subject of analysis rather than as a language to be spoken, the reader will require some familiarity with linguistics. Any of these books will be useful as points of departure:

Bolinger, Dwight. *Aspects of Language.* New York: Harcourt, Brace and World, 1968.

Fromkin, Victoria, and Robert Rodman. *An Introduction to Language.* 2d ed. New York: Holt, Rinehart and Winston, 1978.

Robins, R.H. *General Linguistics: An Introductory Survey.* 2d ed. London: Longmans, 1971.

As an introduction to the study of language for the more advanced reader, Bloomfield's *Language* remains unsurpassed:

Bloomfield, Leonard. *Language.* New York: Holt, Rinehart and Winston, 1933.

More Technical Works on Cree

Since Cree is a member of the Algonquian family of languages, the standard reference works on Algonquian include linguistic books and articles about Cree. *Algonquian Linguistics* appears at irregular intervals; the *Papers of the Algonquian Conference* have been issued annually since 1975.

> *Algonquian Linguistics.* Thunder Bay, Ontario: Native Teacher Education Programme, Lakehead University.

> *Papers of the Seventh [Eighth, . . .] Algonquian Conference.* Ottawa: Department of Linguistics, Carleton University, 1975 [1976, . . .].

> Pentland, David H., C. Douglas Ellis, Carol A. Simpson, and H. Christoph Wolfart. *A Bibliography of Algonquian Linguistics.* University of Manitoba Anthropology Papers 11. Winnipeg: Department of Anthropology, University of Manitoba, 1974.

Most of the titles listed in this section (or included in the above reference works) will be difficult to appreciate without at least some background in linguistics.

> Bloomfield, Leonard. "The Plains Cree Language." In *International Congress of Americanists, Proceedings* 22, part 2. 427–31. Rome, 1928.

> Ellis, C. Douglas. "Tagmemic Analysis of a Restricted Cree Text." *Journal of the Canadian Linguistic Association* 6. 35–59. (1960).

> ——. "The So-Called Interrogative Order in Cree." *International Journal of American Linguistics* 27. 119–124. (1961)

> ——. "Cree Verb Paradigms." *International Journal of American Linguistics* 37. 76–95. (1971).
> A survey of Cree verb forms based on Moose Cree and the Swampy Cree of Fort Albany.

Longacre, Robert E. "Quality and Quantity in Cree Vowels." *Journal of the Canadian Linguistic Association* 3. 66–70. (1956).

Wolfart, H. Christoph. *Plains Cree: A Grammatical Study.* American Philosophical Society, Transactions, vol. 63, part 5. Philadelphia: American Philosophical Society, 1973.
This study may be used as a reference grammar.

——. "How Many Obviatives: Sense and Reference in a Cree Verb Paradigm." *Linguistic Studies of Native Canada.* Edited by E.-D. Cook and J. Kaye. 255–72. Vancouver: University of British Columbia Press, 1978.

Two volumes of Plains Cree texts have been published along with English translations.* These texts, which were collected in Saskatchewan in 1925, are presented in an orthography compatible with that used in this book.

Bloomfield, Leonard. *Sacred Stories of the Sweet Grass Cree.* National Museum of Canada, Bulletin 60. Ottawa: The King's Printer, 1930. [Reprinted, New York: AMS Press, 1976.]

——. *Plains Cree Texts.* American Ethnological Society, Publication 16. New York: G.E. Stechert & Co., 1934. [Reprinted. New York: AMS Press, 1974.]

*The cultural and historical background of these texts is outlined in David Mandelbaum's *The Plains Cree: An Ethnographic, Historical, and Comparative Study* (Regina: Canadian Plains Research Centre, University of Regina, 1979).

Difficulties with Books on Cree

Many books on Cree and other North American languages have been written by people whose primary competence lies in such areas as trading, teaching, or missionary work. It is obvious that many of these authors had an impressive command of the language they were writing about, and this is an important point.

At the same time, however, it must be emphasized that language is an immensely complex system of interrelationships, no less complex than any other aspect of human nature. Everyone will agree that a person who breathes is not, by virtue of this fact alone, capable of describing the lung and its function: such a specialized task requires training and experience. While we all are able to *use* language (just as we use our lungs), its scientific description also requires specialized training and experience. A large body of knowledge has been assembled about the details of man's ability to speak and to understand speech, and it seems only reasonable that training in linguistics should be of importance in describing a language.

In view of this fact the achievements of many amateur linguists are indeed remarkable. The grammars of Howse and Lacombe and the dictionaries of Lacombe and Watkins-Faries are valuable documents which deserve to be studied very carefully. However, they cannot be recommended to the student of Cree (even though other dictionaries are not available). In spite of their excellence in some areas, inconsistent orthographies and other basic problems place severe restrictions on their practical usefulness.

Howse, Joseph. *A Grammar of the Cree Language.* London, 1844.

Lacombe, Albert. *Grammaire de la langue des Cris.* Montréal, 1874.

——. *Dictionnaire de la langue des Cris.* Montréal, 1874.

Faries, Richard, ed. *A Dictionary of the Cree Language.* Toronto: Anglican Church of Canada, 1938.
A revised version of E.A. Watkins's dictionary of the same title, published in London in 1865.

While the works just mentioned are of considerable intrinsic value, a number of other books on Cree are now mainly of historical interest. The grammars of Hives, Horden, and Hunter are typical.

Hives, H.E. *Cree Grammar*. Toronto, 1948.

Horden, J. *A Grammar of the Cree Language as Spoken by the Cree Indians of North America*. London, 1881.

Hunter, James. *A Lecture on the Grammatical Construction of the Cree Language*. London, 1875.

Although published only recently, the following work shares all the drawbacks of the earlier dictionaries:

Anderson, Anne. *Plains Cree Dictionary in the "y" Dialect, Revised*. [Edmonton, privately printed,] 1975.

In addition, it yields to an old temptation in an extreme way: instead of collecting Cree words which are actually in use, Anderson largely translates an English school dictionary (Winston) into Cree. Aside from other problems, she thus includes a large number of entries (such as *polka, polo, polygamy, pompadour, poncho, pongee, poor-house* on page 91) which could hardly be more relevant to contemporary Cree culture than specialized terms for the innards of a camel.

In some cases, the lack of linguistic knowledge or guidance is particularly severe, and where this technical deficiency is combined with great dedication (as is obviously true for the next two authors), the results are especially distressing.

Logan, Robert A. "The Precise Speakers." *Beaver*, June 1951.

———. *The Cree Language, As It Appears to Me.* Privately printed, 1958.

———. *Cree Language Structure.* Privately printed, 1964.

Sealey, D. Bruce. "Algonkian Linguistics." *Indians Without Tipis.* Edited by D.B. Sealey and V.J. Kirkness. 73–95. Winnipeg, 1973.

Logan's and Sealey's writings deserve special mention since they are contemporary and have, in the absence of other readily accessible materials, achieved extremely wide distribution (even to the point of being cited and paraphrased in scholarly journals). Unfortunately, however, in the writings of some authors misinformation, misinterpretation, and confusion far outweigh whatever reliable information there may be. Rather than merely being not useful, such works are distinctly harmful.